ELECTRIC STEAMER RECIPE BOOK

Transform Your Kitchen into a Culinary Haven with Simple and Tasty Steam Cooking

~ Phyllis J. Waldrop ~

Electric Steamer Recipe Book

Transform Your Kitchen into a Culinary Haven with Simple and Tasty Steam Cooking

Phyllis J. Waldrop

Copyright © by Phyllis J. Waldrop

All rights reserved. No part of this book may be reproduced, distributed, or transmitted in any form or by any means, including photocopying, recording, or other electronic or mechanical methods, without the prior written permission of the publisher, except in the case of brief quotations embodied in critical reviews and certain other noncommercial uses permitted by copyright law.

Table of content

- Introduction 11
- Introduction to Electric Steamers: 13
- Choosing the Right Electric Steamer: A Comprehensive Guide 17
- Maintaining Your Electric Steamer: A Guide to Prolonging Lifespan and Ensuring Peak Performance 21
- Troubleshooting Electric Steamer Issues: A Comprehensive Guide to Common Problems and Solutions 23
- Unveiling the Green Side of Electric Steamers: A Deep Dive into Energy Efficiency and Eco-Friendly Practices 27
- Tips for using electric steam that is good for the environment: 29
- Innovations in Electric Steam Technology: A Look into Smart Features and Connectivity Options 31
- Electric steamer recipes and cooking tips: Unlocking the Potential of Food 33

BREAKFAST 37

1. Fluffy Steamed Pancakes with Maple Syrup 39
2. Savory Egg Bites with Spinach and Sausage 40
3. Tropical Fruit and Yogurt Parfait 41
4. Steamed Salmon and Cream Cheese Bagels 42
5. Steamed Waffles with Berries 43
6. Steamed Tofu Scramble with Turmeric 44
7. Mini Steamed Quiches with Spinach and Feta 45
8. Steamed Curry and Chickpea Scramble 46
9. Steamed Yogurt and Granola Muffins 47
10. Mini Steamed Frittatas with Cherry Tomatoes 48
11. Steamed Apple Crumble with Greek Yogurt 49
12. Mango and Coconut Steamed Rice Pudding 50
13. Vegetable Fritters with Avocado Salsa 51
14. Steamed Sausage and Sweet Potato 53
15. Poached Eggs on Steamed Spinach 54
16. Cinnamon Spiced Steamed Oatmeal 55
17. Mini Steamed Breakfast Burritos 56
18. Strawberry and Ricotta Steamed Crepes 57
19. Tropical Smoothie Bowl with Steamed Quinoa 58
20. Steamed Banana and Oatmeal Pancakes 59

COMFORT FOOD 61

21. Fluffy Steamed Mac and Cheese 63
22. Steamed Chicken Pot Pie with Puff Pastry Crust 64
23. Savory Steamed Meatloaf with Glazed Carrots 65
24. Sticky Honey Garlic Salmon with Broccoli 66
25. Spicy Korean Beef Bulgogi Bowl with Brown Rice 67
26. Steamed Chicken and Dumplings 69
27. Classic American Cheeseburgers 70
28. Steamed Salmon and Asparagus 71
29. Vegetable Lasagna with Ricotta and Spinach 72
30. Steamed Chicken and Vegetable Curry 74
31. Fluffy White Steamed Buns 75
32. Creamy Polenta with Grilled Vegetables 76
33. Steamed Shrimp Wontons 77
34. Sticky Toffee Pudding 79
35. Steamed Apple and Cranberry Crumble 81
36. Savory Beef Stew with Root Vegetables 82
37. Steamed Chicken and Vegetable Potpourri 83

- 38. Tropical Fruit and Coconut Cream Steamed 84
- 39. Comforting Steamed Chicken Noodle Soup 85
- 40. Cinnamon Raisin Steamed Buns 86

SIDES DISHES 87

- 41. Rainbow Veggie Spring Rolls 89
- 42. Steamed Asparagus with Lemon and Parmesan 90
- 43. Creamy Garlic Mashed Potatoes 91
- 44. Honey Sriracha Brussels Sprouts 92
- 45. Steamed Quinoa with Herbs and Nuts 93
- 46. Savory Sun-kissed Broccolini 94
- 47. Garlicky Sichuan Edamame with Toasted Sesame 95
- 48. Steamed Corn on the Cob with Garlic Herb 96
- 49. Mediterranean Bliss with Capers and Feta 97
- 50. Classic Garlicky Beans with Toasted Almonds 98
- 51. Honey Balsamic Glazed Sweet Potatoes 99
- 52. Provençal Sunshine with Fresh Herbs 100
- 53. Provençal Sun-Kissed Spinach 101
- 54. Steamed Cauliflower Rice with Parmesan 102
- 55. Honey Glazed Carrots with Pecans 103
- 56. Steamed Broccoli with Sesame Ginger 104
- 57. Roasted Pumpkin and Feta Salad 105
- 58. Steamed Zucchini and Yellow Squash 107
- 59. Steamed Artichokes with Lemon Butter Dip 108
- 60. Grilled Fruit Skewers with Honey Yogurt 110

MAIN COURSES 111

- 61. Spicy Korean Beef Bulgogi Bowl 113
- 62. Honey Garlic Salmon with Broccoli 115
- 63. Steamed Chicken and Dumplings 116
- 64. Steamed Dim Sum 118
- 65. Lemon Garlic Chicken and Asparagus 119
- 66. Mediterranean Bliss with Lemon, Tomatoes 120
- 67. Spicy Black Bean Burgers 121
- 68. Classic Teriyaki with Sesame and Toasted Almonds 122
- 69. Thai Fusion Bliss with Sweet Chili 123
- 70. Savory Meatloaf with Herb Glaze 125
- 71. Provencal Sunshine with Creamy Coconut 126
- 72. Mediterranean Delight with Sun-Dried Tomatoes 127
- 73. Thai Curry with Vegetables and Tofu 128
- 74. Chicken Pot Pie with Puff Pastry Crust 130
- 75. Moroccan Chicken Tagine with Couscous 132
- 76. Shrimp and Vegetable Spring Rolls 133
- 77. Mediterranean Sun-Kissed Chicken 135
- 78. Vegetable Lasagna with Ricotta 136
- 79. Spicy Cajun Shrimp Boil with Corn and Potatoes 138
- 80. Fluffy White Steamed Buns 139

INTERNATIONAL FLAVORS 141

- 81. Vietnamese Bun Chay 143
- 82. Japanese Gyoza with Sesame Ginger Dipping Sauce 145
- 83. Korean Japchae 147
- 84. Thai Green Curry with Coconut Milk 149

85. Chinese Steamed Fish with Ginger 150
86. Chicken Tikka Masala 151
87. Moroccan Chicken Tagine with Couscous 152
88. Turkish Manti Dumplings 154
89. Ethiopian Vegan Misir Wat Stew 156
90. Lebanese Steamed Kibbeh Meatballs 158
91. Italian Steamed Mussels with White Wine 160
92. Greek Stuffed Grape Leaves 161
93. Spanish Steamed Bacalao with Romesco 162
94. French Bouillabaisse 163
95. German Steamed Dumplings with Sauerkraut 165
96. Mexican Steamed Tamales with Chicken 167
97. Brazilian Moqueca de Peixe 169
98. Cuban Ropa Vieja 171
99. Peruvian Steamed Ceviche 173
100. Argentinian Steamed Empanadas 174

DESKTOP & SWEET ENDINGS 177

101. Steamed Apple Crumble with Vanilla Ice Cream 179
102. Tropical Fruit and Yogurt Parfait 180
103. Sticky Rice Mango Pudding with Coconut Cream 181
104. Steamed Berries with Honey and Mint 182
105. Poached Peaches with Vanilla Bean Yogurt 183
106. Chocolate Chip Banana Bread 184
107. Steamed Molten Lava Cakes 185
108. Dark Chocolate Steamed Pudding 186
109. Steamed Banana Muffins 188
110. Strawberry and Ricotta Steamed Crepes 189
111. Steamed Baklava with Rosewater 190
112. Japanese Green Tea Mochi with Red Bean Paste 192
113. French Steamed Clafoutis 193
114. Italian Steamed Ricotta Cheesecake 194
115. Orange Blossom Steamed Rice Pudding 195
116. Steamed Fruit Cobbler with Berries, Peaches 196
117. Honey Glazed Carrots with Pecans 197
118. Steamed Yogurt and Granola Muffins 198
119. Spiced Pears with Vanilla Bean Sauce 199
120. Steamed Frittatas with Cherry Tomatoes 201

INTRODUCTION

Welcome to "Electric Steamer Recipe Book: Transform Your Kitchen into a Culinary Haven with Simple and Tasty Steam Cooking" by Phyllis J. Waldrop. Within the pages of this culinary compendium, embark on a delightful journey that promises to revolutionize your home cooking through the magic of steam.

With 120 meticulously curated recipes, this book covers a wide array of culinary delights across six distinct categories. Begin your day on a savory note with our Breakfast selection, where steam transforms the ordinary into extraordinary. Seek solace in the warmth of Comfort Food recipes that bring a sense of nostalgia and satisfaction to your table. Elevate your meals with innovative and delectable sides dishes that perfectly complement any main course.

Discover the heart of your dining experience in our Main Courses section, where steam takes center stage to create dishes that are not only delicious but also health-conscious. Embark on a global culinary adventure with International Flavors, bringing the world's tastes and aromas into your kitchen. Conclude your meals on a sweet note with our Desserts & Sweet Endings, where the simplicity of steam transforms ordinary desserts into extraordinary indulgences.

As the author, Phyllis J. Waldrop, guides you through this culinary exploration, you'll find that the electric steamer is more than just a kitchen appliance; it's a gateway to a world of culinary creativity and healthful cooking. Each recipe is crafted to showcase the simplicity, speed, and unparalleled flavor that steam brings to the table.

Whether you're a seasoned chef or a novice in the kitchen, this book offers something for everyone. Let the aromatic wonders of steam cooking fill your kitchen, transforming it into a haven of culinary delights. Get ready to savor the simplicity and taste the transformation as you embark on an unforgettable journey with "Electric Steamer Recipe Book."

Electric steamers have become indispensable appliances in modern households, offering efficient and healthy cooking and garment care solutions. In this comprehensive overview, we will delve into the various types of electric steamers available in the market, providing an in-depth exploration of their features, functions, and the pros and cons associated with each type.

INTRODUCTION TO ELECTRIC STEAMERS:

Electric steamers use steam to cook food or get rid of wrinkles in clothes, so you don't need oil or dangerous chemicals. People like these multipurpose appliances because they work well, are simple to use, and keep foods' nutritional value. Let's look at the different kinds of electric steamers and the different ways they can be used.

1. Food steamers:

In short, food steamers, which are sometimes called electric steam cookers, use steam to cook different kinds of food. These appliances usually have more than one tier or compartment, which lets people steam different foods at the same time without mixing the flavors.

Pros:

- Keeping the nutrients: Steaming is better than boiling or frying at keeping the vitamins and minerals in food.
- Flexible: It's great for cooking fish, chicken, vegetables, and even desserts.
- Efficiency: Multiple compartments let you cook different foods at the same time.

Cons:

- Fewer cooking options: They work well for steaming but might need to be right for frying or baking.
- Size Limitations: Each compartment may not have enough space for bigger meals because it is small.

2. Steam irons for clothes:

In short, garment steamers are made to get rid of wrinkles and take care of fabrics. These gadgets use steam to loosen up fabric fibers, which means you don't need an ironing board to get rid of wrinkles.

Pros:

- Gentle on Fabrics: This iron is great for delicate fabrics that might get damaged by regular ironing.
- Fast and Easy: Steamers are easier to use and faster than irons, especially for getting rid of light wrinkles.

Versatility: It can be used on silk, wool, and other fabrics.

Cons:

- Not Good for Heavy-Duty Jobs: It might not work as well on heavy fabrics or wrinkles that are set in deep.
- Size of the Water Tank: Smaller tanks may need to be refilled more often for bigger jobs.

3. Multi-use steamers:

Multi-functional steamers have the features of both food and garment steamers, making them a flexible choice for homes that want one appliance that can do many different things.

Pros:

- Saving space: Putting multiple functions into one device cuts down on the need for extra ones.
- Savings: This is cheaper than buying separate steamers for food and clothes.
- Time-saving: Users can easily switch from steaming food to washing clothes.

Cons:

- Specific Design: Some models might not be as good at one task as appliances that are made just for that task.
- Complications: Because they have so many features, multi-functional steamers may require more work to learn how to use.

4. Stick-on steamers:

Overview: Handheld steamers are small, portable machines that are mostly used for steaming clothes. They're small and light, so you can use them anywhere.

Pros:

- They're small and light, which makes them great for traveling.
- Fast Heat-Up: Handheld steamers often heat up quickly so they can be used right away.
- Spot cleaning is good for cleaning specific parts of clothes.

Cons:

- Smaller water tanks may need to be refilled more often for bigger jobs.
- Not to Be Used Often: Best for quick touch-ups rather than getting rid of a lot of wrinkles.

5. Steamers for business:

Commercial steamers are heavy-duty machines made for use in factories or on a large scale. These steamers can handle a lot of food and are often found in professional kitchens.

Pros:

- High Capacity: They are designed to hold a lot of food, which makes them perfect for commercial kitchens.
- Durability: Made with strong materials that will last through a lot of use.
- Customization: Some models come with more advanced control options for precise cooking.

Cons:

- Size and Weight: They're big and heavy, so small kitchens and homes can't use them.
- Cost: Private steamers are usually less expensive than commercial ones.

In the end,

Additionally, electric steamers have changed over time to meet the needs of many individuals, from chefs seeking healthier ways to cook to regular people seeking quick and simple methods to clean their clothes. Picking the right electric steamer depends on your personal preferences, way of life, and the reason for the steamer.

When buying an electric steamer, people should carefully think about things like capacity, versatility, and extra features. Food steamers make nutritious meals, garment steamers get rid of wrinkles in clothes, and all-in-one multi-functional steamers make our lives easier. These appliances are changing how we cook and care for our things. As technology gets better, we can expect even more changes to be made to how electric steamers are made, making them even more useful and efficient in the years to come.

CHOOSING THE RIGHT ELECTRIC STEAMER: A COMPREHENSIVE GUIDE

Electric steamers are common in modern kitchens because they make cooking easy and healthy. You need to carefully think about a lot of different things when choosing the right electric steamer, whether you want a food steamer, a garment steamer, or a unit that can do more than one thing. This detailed guide will talk about the most important things to consider when buying an electric steamer, focusing on size and capacity.

When buying an electric steamer, things you should think about are:

What kind of steamer is it?

1. Food Steamer:

If your main goal is to make healthy meals with little work, you should get a food steamer. For more options, look for features like multiple tiers and settings that can be programmed.

2. Garment Steamer:

A garment steamer is necessary to get clothes dry and wrinkle-free without having to iron them. For easier portability, think about handheld models. For bigger jobs, think about standing models.

3. Multi-Functional Steamer:

A multi-functional steamer might be the right choice if you want an appliance that can cook and maintain clothes.

Kitchen Space:

Size and Plans: Check to see how much space you have in your kitchen. Choose a small model or steamer that is easy to store when not in use if you have limited counter space.

If you plan to move the steamer around a lot, think about how heavy it is and how it's made. People with small kitchens or little storage space will love these models because they are small and light.

Families should choose a steamer whose capacity matches their number of people. For larger families, steamers with more than one level or a bigger overall capacity may be needed to cook enough food at once.

One or More Compartments: Some steamers only have one compartment, while others have more than one. With a multi-compartment steamer, you can cook different foods at the same time without transferring the flavors.

4. Affordability:

Control Panel: An electric steamer should have an easy-to-use control panel. Digital screens and settings that can be programmed make cooking easier and more accurate.

Water Tank: Check to see how easy it is to fill and empty the water tank. Transparent reservoirs make it easy to see how much water is in them while they are being used.

5. Easy to Clean and Maintain:

Parts That Can Go in the Dishwasher: Choose steamers that have parts that can go in the dishwasher for easy cleaning. Having parts that can be taken off and put back on makes maintenance easier.

Features for Descale: Some steamers have features for descaling that keep mineral deposits from building up over time. This keeps the machine running at its best and for as long as possible.

6. Extra Highlights:

Timers and Delay Start: Look for models with programmable timers and delay start options for added convenience. This will let you set up the steamer ahead of time.

Function to Keep Warm: This feature helps keep your food at the right temperature until you're ready to serve it.

Size and Capacity Things to Think About:

Plan your meals and how often you'll use the steamer. If you want to use it often, pick a size that fits the amount of food you usually cook at once to avoid making multiple batches.

Use Occasional: If you only use your steamer occasionally, a smaller one might be enough, saving you space in your kitchen.

Family Size: Small Families or Individuals: Smaller, more compact steamers are good for individuals or small families.

Medium to Large Families: Steamers with more than one level or a bigger overall capacity may be better for larger families.

Flexibility: Single or Multi-Compartment: Single-compartment steamers are best for certain dishes, while multi-compartment models can cook a variety of meals at the same time.

Storage: Compact Design: If you have a limited amount of room for storage, pick a small steamer that can be put away easily in cabinets or on shelves when not in use.

In the end,

You need to carefully think about your needs and preferences in order to choose the right electric steamer. Whether you care more about how quickly you cook, how well your clothes stay clean, or a mix of the two, size, capacity, and extra features will help you find a steamer that fits your needs. With the right choice, you can start a culinary journey that is convenient and makes your meals healthier while ensuring your clothes look great.

MAINTAINING YOUR ELECTRIC STEAMER: A GUIDE TO PROLONGING LIFESPAN AND ENSURING PEAK PERFORMANCE

Electric steamers have changed the way we cook by giving us a quick and healthy alternative to the old ways of doing things. Make sure your electric steamer works well and lasts a long time by cleaning and maintaining it properly. This guide will show you how to properly clean and descale your electric steamer and give you maintenance tips to keep it in great shape.

Maintenance Tips to Make It Last Longer:

- Do regular checks on the power cord and plug. Make sure the power cord doesn't have any frays or wires that are showing. Check to see if the plug is broken in any way.
- Take care of your water reservoir by emptying it every time you use it: Fill up the water tank every time you use it so that mold and bacteria don't grow in it.

Use Distilled Water:

- If the water in your area is hard, you should use distilled water to keep minerals from building up in the reservoir.

Routine for descale:

Set up a schedule for descaling: Set up a routine for descaling based on how hard your water is. Mineral deposits can form in hard water, which can make the steamer work less well.

Vinegar or Descaling Solution should be used: Make a solution with white vinegar and water, or use a store-bought descaler that the manufacturer recommends.

Clean the outside:

- Use a damp cloth to wipe the outside with water to remove any food splatters or leftovers.
- Avoid Abrasive Cleaners: Do not apply abrasive cleaners on the steamer because they could damage the finish.

Check the steam trays and baskets:

- Get Rid of Residue: Take out and clean the steam baskets and trays after each use to keep them from getting dirty.
- Safe for the dishwasher: Put parts that can be taken off in the dishwasher to make things easier.
- Check the seals and gaskets for damage and wear: Check seals and gaskets often for damage or signs of wear. If you need to, replace it to keep the seal working right.

Steps for Cleaning and Descale:

- Rinsing and emptying: Unplug the steamer. To be safe, you should always unplug the steamer before cleaning it.
- Empty the Water Reservoir: Throw away any water that is still in the reservoir and trays.

Cleaning the Water Tank:

- Solution of vinegar: Fill a bowl with equal parts white vinegar and water. Put the solution in the tank and wait 15 to 30 minutes.
- Gentle Scrub: Scrub the inside of the reservoir with a soft brush or sponge, paying special attention to places where minerals have built up.
- Rinse Very Well: To get rid of any vinegar residue, rinse the reservoir well with clean water.

To clean baskets and trays, soak them in warm, soapy water. Take the trays and baskets out of the steamer and soak them in warm, soapy water.

- Scrub gently: To get rid of any food particles or residue, apply a brush or sponge that doesn't scratch.
- Dishwasher Option: If these parts can go in the dishwasher, do so for a thorough cleaning.
- Descaling Steps: Make the descaling solution: Follow the directions on the bottle to mix the right amount of vinegar or descaling solution with water.
- Run the Steamer: Add the solution to the water tank and let the steamer go through its full cycle.
- Rinse with Clean Water: Once the scale is off, run clean water through the steamer to get rid of any leftover descaler.
- 5. Clean the outside with a damp cloth. Use a damp cloth to wipe down the outside to get rid of any spills or stains.
- To dry completely: Before plugging the steamer back in, make sure it is completely dry.

By keeping up with these cleaning and maintenance tips, you can make your electric steamer last longer and keep it working at its best. Regular maintenance keeps the cooking area clean and stops mineral deposits from building up, which can make your appliance less effective. Your electric steamer will be a useful and reliable kitchen appliance for many years to come if you take care of it and keep it in good shape.

TROUBLESHOOTING ELECTRIC STEAMER ISSUES: A COMPREHENSIVE GUIDE TO COMMON PROBLEMS AND SOLUTIONS

Electric steamers are now necessary kitchen tools because they make cooking meals healthy and quick. However, electric steamers can have problems that stop them from working properly like any other electronic device. In this detailed guide, we'll talk about common issues with electric steamers and give you useful advice on fixing problems like unevenly steaming or water leaking.

Finding Issues That Arise Often:

Possible Reasons:

- The food in the steamer baskets needed to be spread out evenly.
- Pipes or vents for steam that are blocked.
- Heaters that aren't even.
- How to Fix Problems:

Rearrange the Food: Make sure that the food is spread out evenly in the steamer baskets so that the steam can flow freely.

Clean the Steam Vents: Use a small brush or toothpick to clear out any clogs in the steam vents or channels.

Check the Heating Elements: If you can, look at the heating elements to see if they are broken or not working right. If you need help from a professional, contact the manufacturer.

Water Leaks:

Possible Reasons:

- Seals that are broken or worn out.
- Putting too much water in the reservoir.
- Not putting together the parts correctly.
- How to Fix Problems:

Check the Seals: Look for any signs of damage or wear on the seals and gaskets. If you need to, replace them to make sure the seal works right.

Refrain from overfilling: Keep the water level in the reservoir above what is recommended. If you overfill, water could leak out while the machine is running.

Proper Assembly: Make sure that all of the parts are put together correctly, including the steam baskets and trays. If the parts are not put together correctly, water could leak out of the steamer.

Not Enough Steam Production:

Possible Reasons:

- Minerals get stuck in the heating element.
- The reservoir needs more water.
- Heating element is broken.
- How to Fix Problems:

Descale the Steamer: If the steamer's output drops, use a descaling solution or a vinegar-and-water mix to clean it. To remove scale, follow the manufacturer's instructions.

Check the Water Level: Ensure the reservoir has enough water. Some steamers may need a certain amount of water to work at their best.

Checking the Heating Element: If descaling doesn't make more steam, check the heating element for damage. If you need to, replace the element.

Controls or displays that don't work right:

Possible reasons:

- Electricity problems.
- The control panel is broken.
- Issues with the power supply.
- How to Fix Problems:

Check the power source: Ensure the steamer is properly plugged in and the power source works. To be sure, plug in something else to the outlet.

Start the steamer up again: Do not use the steamer for a while, then turn it back on. There are times when this can reset the control panel.

Talk to customer service: If the problem keeps happening, call the manufacturer's customer service for help with diagnosing the control panel or looking into possible repairs.

Preventive Steps:

To keep your electric steamer in good shape and avoid common problems, you might want to take the following precautions:

Regular Descaling: To keep minerals from building up in the heating element and steam pathways, schedule regular descaling.

How to Store It: When not in use, keep the electric steamer in a dry, cool place to keep the electrical parts from breaking down.

Gentle Handling: To keep things from getting worn out, handle things sparingly, especially when putting them together or taking them apart.

Follow the User Manual: Read and follow the manufacturer's instructions in the user manual about how much water to use, where to put food, and how to keep the machine in good shape.

You can make sure that your electric steamer stays a reliable and useful kitchen tool by quickly fixing common problems and taking preventative steps. Giving your appliance regular care and attention will not only fix problems but it will also help it last longer so you can enjoy healthy cooking without any hassle for years to come.

UNVEILING THE GREEN SIDE OF ELECTRIC STEAMERS: A DEEP DIVE INTO ENERGY EFFICIENCY AND ECO-FRIENDLY PRACTICES

Electric steamers have become popular as helpful kitchen tools that save time and are better for the environment. This article looks into energy efficiency by comparing different electric steamers and showing how using steam for cooking can be eco-friendly.

Comparing how much energy electric steamers use:

Feature that saves energy:

Intelligent Controls: A lot of new electric steamers have intelligent controls that make the best use of energy based on the type and amount of food being cooked.

Programmable Timer: Being able to set exact cooking times helps cut down on energy use that isn't necessary.

Instant Heat Technology: Some electric steamers use this technology to speed up the time it takes to reach the right cooking temperature, which saves energy in the long run.

Variable Power Settings: Changeable power settings let people adjust how much energy they use based on the type of food they are cooking.

Versatility and multiple uses:

Combination Cooking: Electric steamers that can do more than one thing (like steaming, baking, etc.) can save energy because they don't need to be used separately.

Insulation and Heat Retention: Efficient Insulation: Chambers in well-insulated steamers can keep heat better, using less energy to keep the food at the right temperature.

Design with Two Layers: Some models have containers or baskets stacked on each other, which keeps heat in even better.

Easy-to-Use Controls: Intuitive Interfaces: Electric steamers with easy-to-use controls make it easier for people to use the appliance efficiently, so mistakes don't cause extra energy use.

TIPS FOR USING ELECTRIC STEAM THAT IS GOOD FOR THE ENVIRONMENT:

Save water:

Use steaming water for other things. Instead of throwing away water after steaming, use it to water plants or do other things around the house.

Whole Food Cooking:

If you want to reduce the amount of waste caused by packaging, choose whole-food cooking instead of processed or pre-packaged foods.

Plan your meals so you have few leftovers, and devise creative ways to use any extra food.

Choose sustainable ingredients:

To lower the damage that food production does to the environment, choose ingredients that are organic, locally sourced, and produced in a way that doesn't harm the environment.

Tips for cooking that use less energy:

- Batch cooking: To get the most out of your energy, cook meals in bulk and store them for later use.
- How to Use Lids: Putting lids on steamers and other cookware helps keep heat in, which speeds up the cooking process and uses less energy.

Think about the energy source:

- Usage of Renewable Energy: If solar or wind power is more common in your area, use electric steamers during those times.

Proper maintenance for long life:

- Regular descaling: Regularly descaling your steamer improves performance and ensures it works efficiently, so you don't have to use as much extra energy.

Electric steamers have brought the way we cook up to date, and they have also made big steps toward more energy-efficient and environmentally friendly cooking. As consumers, we can help make kitchens more sustainable and eco-friendly by using these technologies and cooking with more care. By using electric steamers that use less energy and doing things that are better for the environment, we can enjoy tasty meals while reducing our carbon footprint and making the future of food greener.

INNOVATIONS IN ELECTRIC STEAM TECHNOLOGY: A LOOK INTO SMART FEATURES AND CONNECTIVITY OPTIONS

Adding cutting-edge technology to electric steamers has made them much better, ushering in a new era of convenience and efficiency in the kitchen. In this article, we'll look at the newest developments in electric steamer technology, focusing on the smart features and connectivity options that have made these appliances smart cooking partners.

1. New developments in electric steamer technology:

- Touchscreen Interfaces for Smart Controls: Many new electric steamers have easy-to-use touchscreen interfaces that let users quickly switch between settings and cooking programs.
- App Integration: Some models can connect to a smartphone, which lets users control and keep an eye on the steamer from afar using special mobile apps.

2. Sensor Technology:

- Food Recognition Sensors: More advanced sensors can automatically tell what kind of food is being cooked and change the temperature and cooking time to get the best results.
- Water Level Sensors: Smart steamers can tell when the water level is low and let users know when it's time to refill, which makes sure the cooking process goes smoothly.

3. Connectivity Options:

- Wi-Fi Connectivity: Electric steamers that can connect to Wi-Fi can easily work with smart home systems, letting you control them with your voice and automate tasks.
- Bluetooth Connectivity: Steamers that have Bluetooth make it easy to connect to smartphones and tablets, which makes the whole experience better for the user.

4. Precise Cooking:

- Temperature Control: Electric steamers now have precise temperature control, which lets people change the way they cook for different recipes.
- Programmable Settings: Users can get consistent, perfect steaming results every time with programmable settings for different foods and ingredients.

Multifunctional Electric Steamers: Looking at Their Uses Aside from Cooking

Electric steamers have gone beyond their traditional roles in the kitchen. Multifunctional models can do many things besides just cooking. Let's look into the innovative world of electric steamers that can do more than one thing, both in and out of the kitchen.

A Look at Steamers That Can Do More Than One Thing:

1. Combo for cooking and ironing:

Two Chambers: Some multifunctional steamers have separate areas for cooking and ironing, making them a convenient all-in-one choice for people who are short on time.

Adjustable Settings: It's easy for users to switch between cooking and ironing modes, and each has its own settings that make it work best.

Thoughts and suggestions on flexible models:

1. Philips All-in-One Cooker: Many types of cooking can be done with this steamer, such as steaming, pressure cooking, and slow cooking. It has a digital screen and settings that can be programmed.

User Feedback: Users like how easy it is to use and how it makes it possible to make a wide range of dishes.

2. Rowenta IXEO All-in-One Iron and Steamer: This innovative appliance is both an ironing board and a garment steamer, making it a useful tool for caring for clothes. It can be used on a wide range of fabrics and has several steam settings.

User Feedback: Reviews talk about how well it gets rid of wrinkles and how convenient it is that it has an ironing board built in.

Electric steamers can be used in creative ways. Applications Not Usually Used.

In addition to their usual use in cooking, electric steamers are useful in a lot of different ways. Today, let's look at some creative and unusual ways to use these appliances to show their flexibility.

Unexpected Ways to Use Your Electric Steamer:

1. Artichoke Blossom: To make this dish, steam whole artichokes until they are soft, then carefully spread the leaves out to make it look like a flower in bloom. Pair with dipping sauce for a unique and eye-catching starter.

2. Steamed buns made at home: You can use the steamer to make homemade steamed buns that are soft, fluffy, and filled with sweet or savory things. A delightful change from the usual way of baking.

3. Infused Steam Cocktails: To make these, use the steamer to add flavors to the cocktails. You can get essential oils from fruits, herbs, or spices by steaming them. These oils will make your favorite drinks smell and taste better.

ELECTRIC STEAMER RECIPES AND COOKING TIPS: UNLOCKING THE POTENTIAL OF FOOD

Electric steamers are a quick and healthy way to cook food. Find electric steamer-friendly recipe ideas as well as cooking tips and tricks to get the most out of these innovative kitchen appliances.

Here are some recipe ideas that are perfect for electric steamers:

1. Salmon and Asparagus Parcels: Fillets of salmon, asparagus, and a drizzle of lemon juice should be put into separate parcels. Steaming makes a dish quick, tasty, and easy to clean up.

2. Stuffed peppers with quinoa and vegetables: Fill bell peppers with a mixture of quinoa, diced vegetables, and spices. Steam the peppers until they are soft for a healthy and colorful meal.

How to get the best results when cooking:

1. Adding Layers of Flavor: Tip: To add more flavors while cooking, try putting herbs, citrus slices, or aromatics between the layers of food in the steamer.

2. Timing and Order: Tip: Plan the order of the things that will be steamed based on how long they take to cook. Start with things that take longer to cook and add things that cook faster later so that everything is done at the same time.

Guidelines for Safe Use of Electric Steamers: Safety Precautions

Electric steamers are useful and easy to use, but it is very important to make sure they are used safely. Learn about important safety tips and common safety features in modern electric steamers to ensure a safe cooking experience.

Tips on how to use electric steamers safely:

1. Read the instructions:

- Be careful: Read the user manual to learn the specific safety instructions the manufacturer gave you.

2. The right source of power:

- Care: Make sure the steamer is hooked up to a power source that works with it, as described in the user manual. If it's not suggested, don't use extension cords.

Modern electric steamers usually have these safety features:

Electronic steamers often have an automatic shut-off feature that stops the machine when the cooking cycle is over, or the water tank is empty.

2. Cool-Touch Exterior: A feature of modern steamers is that the outside stays cool to the touch while they're working, which keeps people from getting burned.

Compared to Other Ways of Cooking: Electric steamers vs. more traditional ways of cooking

Electric steamers have changed how meals are made, but how do they compare to old-fashioned cooking methods in terms of taste and nutrition? Let's look at the pros and cons of electric steamers compared to more traditional methods used in the kitchen.

Electric steamers have these pros:

1. Keeps more of the food's nutrients: Steaming is known to do this better than boiling or frying, which makes electric steamers a great choice for people who care about their health.

Advantage: Electric steamers often use less energy than other ways of cooking because they use steam to cook food quickly and well.

Not so good things about electric steamers:

1. Limited Cooking Styles: This is a disadvantage: electric steamers are great for steaming, but they might need to be right for other cooking styles, like frying or baking. This makes them less flexible.

2. Limits on Capacity:

Cons: Some electric steamers may need help holding a lot of food, which could be a problem when cooking for many people.

Reviews and suggestions from users: Advice from People Who Have Been There

Finding out about the real-life experiences of electric steamer users can tell you a lot about how well they work and how reliable they are. This part has reviews from real people who have used popular electric steamers. These reviews give tips and suggestions from people who have used the appliances.

Thoughts from Long-Term Users:

1. Instant Pot Electric Steamers: User Insight: People who have used Instant Pot electric steamers often say how well and how many dishes they can cook quickly and easily. Positive feedback is given for the multifunctionality and easy-to-use interface.

2. Breville SmartSteam Electric Steamer: What Users Think: The Breville SmartSteam has been praised for its precise cooking capabilities, and users have said that they like how well it works with their smartphones.

Conclusion: Electric steamers make cooking more enjoyable.

Electric steamers have gone beyond their original purposes and become smart, flexible, and environmentally friendly kitchen helpers. Electric steamers are changing the way people cook with their smart features, ability to do more than one thing at once, creative uses, and safety features. The electric steamer is a great example of how modern kitchens can be innovative and efficient, whether you're a health-conscious person looking for meals that are high in nutrients or a tech-savvy home chef who likes to use smart kitchen tools. Electric steamers are going to be very important in the future of home cooking because they are getting better all the time and adding more features.

BREAKFAST

1. FLUFFY STEAMED PANCAKES WITH MAPLE SYRUP

Prep Time: 10 minutes | Cook Time: 15 minutes

Total Time: 25 minutes

Servings: 6-8 pancakes

Ingredients

- 1/4 tsp salt
- 2 tsp baking powder
- 1 cup of all-purpose flour
- 1 egg
- 1 tbsp sugar
- 1 tbsp melted butter, plus extra for greasing the steamer
- 1 cup of milk
- Fresh berries (optional)
- Maple syrup (optional)

Instructions

1. In a large bowl, mix together the flour, baking powder, salt, and sugar. Use a whisk to mix them together.
2. In a different bowl, mix the milk, egg, and melted butter together with a whisk.
3. Blend the wet and dry ingredients together with a whisk until they are just mixed. Don't mix too much. Butter should be used to grease the steamer baskets.
4. Make sure there is enough room for the pancakes to rise when you pour the batter into the steamer baskets.
5. In a steamer pot with an inch of water, put the steamer baskets.
6. When the water starts to boil, turn down the heat and cover the pot.
7. Stick a toothpick in the middle of one and steam it for 10 to 15 minutes, or until it comes out clean. Repeat with the rest of the batter.
8. If you'd like, you can serve the pancakes warm with fresh berries and maple syrup.

2. SAVORY EGG BITES WITH SPINACH AND SAUSAGE

Prep Time: 10 minutes | Cook Time: 15 minutes

Total Time: 25 minutes

Servings: 12-14 egg bites

Ingredients

- Cooking spray
- 6 eggs
- 1/4 cup of milk
- 1/4 cup of shredded cheese (cheddar, mozzarella, or your preference)
- 1/4 tsp salt
- Pinch of red pepper flakes (optional)
- 1/4 cup of chopped cooked sausage
- 1/4 tsp black pepper
- 1/2 cup of chopped fresh spinach

Instructions

1. Warm up your electric steamer.
2. Cover a silicone muffin tin or small ramekins with cooking spray.
3. Whisk the eggs and milk together in a large bowl until they are well mixed.
4. You can add cheese, spinach, salt, pepper, cooked sausage and red pepper flakes if you want. Spread the egg mix out evenly in the muffin tins or ramekins.
5. Put the pan in the steamer basket and steam for 15 to 20 minutes or until the egg bites are set. Before you serve the egg bites, let them cool down a bit.

3. TROPICAL FRUIT AND YOGURT PARFAIT

Prep Time: 5 minutes | Cook Time: 0 minutes

Total Time: 5 minutes

Servings: 1-2 parfaits

Ingredients

- 1/4 cup of sliced mango
- 1/4 cup of diced kiwi
- 1/2 cup of plain Greek yogurt
- 1/4 cup of chopped pineapple
- 1/4 cup of granola (optional)
- Honey or drizzle of coconut milk (optional)
- Mint leaves for garnish (optional)

Instructions

1. You can steam the fruit for a few minutes in your electric steamer basket before chopping it if you'd like it a little softer. Add a few tbsp of water to the bottom of the basket so that the food can steam without touching it.
2. Put the Greek yogurt in a bowl or parfait glass and layer it up.
3. Add the chopped fruits on top, making sure they are spread out evenly.
4. If you want, sprinkle granola on top.
5. Add mint leaves as a garnish and, if you want, drizzle with honey or coconut milk.

4. STEAMED SALMON AND CREAM CHEESE BAGELS

Prep Time: 10 minutes | Cook Time: 12-15 minutes

Total Time: 25 minutes

Servings: 2

Ingredients

- 1 tbsp fresh dill, chopped (optional)
- 2 bagels, halved
- 1/4 tsp lemon juice (optional)
- 4 ounces (113g) smoked salmon, thinly sliced
- 4 ounces (113g) cream cheese, softened
- Black pepper to taste

Instructions

1. Put water in your electric steamer and heat it up until it boils.
2. Put cream cheese on both halves of the bagel while you wait. If you want to make the cream cheese taste better, you can add dill and lemon juice to it.
3. Place the buttery smoked salmon slices on top of the cream cheese.
4. Put the bagel halves in the steamer basket and steam for 12 to 15 minutes, or until the cream cheese is just starting to melt and the salmon is warm. As needed, add black pepper.

5. STEAMED WAFFLES WITH BERRIES

Prep Time: 15 minutes | Cook Time: 15-20 minutes

Total Time: 30-35 minutes

Servings: 4-6 waffles

Ingredients

- 2 eggs
- Maple syrup, whipped cream, or yogurt (optional)
- 1/4 tsp salt
- 1 tbsp honey
- 1/2 cup of fresh berries (blueberries, raspberries, strawberries, etc.)
- 1 1/4 cups of milk
- Honey for drizzling (optional)
- 1 tbsp vegetable oil
- 1 1/2 cups of whole wheat flour
- 2 tsp baking powder

Instructions

1. Get your electric waffle maker ready to go.
2. Using a whisk, baking powder, mix the flour and salt together in a large bowl.
3. Separately, mix honey, milk, and eggs in a bowl with an electric mixer.
4. One by one, add the wet ingredients to the dry ones and stir just until everything is combined. Don't mix too much. Combine the vegetable oil with the flour.
5. Fold the fresh berries in slowly.
6. Follow the directions on the package to put batter into a waffle maker that has already been heated.
7. They should be steamed for 5 to 7 minutes on each side, or until they are golden brown and fully cooked. Repeat with the rest of the batter.

6. STEAMED TOFU SCRAMBLE WITH TURMERIC

Prep Time: 10 minutes | Cook Time: 15 minutes

Total Time: 25 minutes

Servings: 2-3

Ingredients

- 1/4 tsp cumin
- 1/4 cup of chopped fresh herbs
- 1/2 tsp ground turmeric
- Pinch of paprika
- 1/2 onion, chopped
- 1 block (14 ounce) extra-firm tofu, drained and pressed
- 1 tbsp olive oil
- 1 clove garlic, minced
- Salt and pepper to taste
- Optional toppings: Nutritional yeast, avocado slices, hot sauce, chopped tomatoes, toasted whole-wheat bread

Instructions

1. Flake the tofu into a bowl with your fingers or a fork. For a smoother scramble, use smaller crumbles. For a more meaty texture, use larger chunks.
2. A big skillet or steamer basket should have olive oil heated up over medium-low heat. The onion will soften after about 5 minutes of cooking.
3. Continue cooking for one more minute after adding the garlic until it smells good.
4. Include paprika, cumin, and turmeric. Wait 30 seconds and let the spices bloom.
5. Spread out the crumbled tofu in a dish by mixing it with the spices.
6. For 10 to 15 minutes, stir the food every now and then while it steams in the skillet or steamer basket. It might need a little water if it gets too dry.
7. To make it taste right, add the fresh herbs and salt and pepper to taste.
8. For a warm serving, top your Steamed Tofu Scramble with whatever you like.

7. MINI STEAMED QUICHES WITH SPINACH AND FETA

Prep Time: 15 minutes | Cook Time: 15-20 minutes

Total Time: 30-35 minutes

Servings: 12-14 quiches

Ingredients

- 1/4 tsp black pepper
- 1 tbsp olive oil
- 1/4 cup of crumbled feta cheese
- 1/2 onion, chopped
- 1 sheet frozen puff pastry, thawed
- 1 clove garlic, minced
- 1/4 tsp salt
- 1/2 cup of milk
- Pinch of nutmeg (optional)
- 3 eggs
- Mini muffin pan greased with non-stick spray
- 4 ounces fresh spinach, chopped

Instructions

1. Preheat your electric steamer. Defrost the puff pastry sheet according to package instructions.
2. Heat olive oil in a small skillet over medium heat. Add onion and cook until softened, about 5 minutes. Add garlic and cook for another minute until fragrant.
3. Stir in the chopped spinach and cook until wilted. Remove from heat and let cool slightly.
4. In a large bowl, whisk together eggs, milk, salt, pepper, and nutmeg (if using).
5. Stir in the cooled spinach mixture and crumbled feta cheese.
6. Cut the puff pastry sheet into squares slightly larger than your mini muffin cups. Gently press the pastry squares into the greased muffin cups, forming little cups.
7. Divide the egg mixture evenly among the pastry cups.
8. Place the muffin pan in the steamer basket and steam for 15-20 minutes, or until the eggs are set and the crust is golden brown. Let the mini quiches cool slightly before serving.

8. STEAMED CURRY AND CHICKPEA SCRAMBLE

Prep Time: 15 minutes | Cook Time: 15 minutes

Total Time: 30 minutes

Servings: 2-3

Ingredients

- 1/2 cup of chopped fresh spinach
- 1 clove garlic, minced
- Fresh cilantro, chopped (for garnish)
- 1/2 tsp ground turmeric
- Naan bread, warmed (for serving)
- 1/2 onion, chopped
- 1/4 cup of milk
- 2 eggs
- 1 tbsp curry paste (your favorite flavor)
- 1/4 tsp chili powder (optional)
- 1 can (15 ounce) chickpeas, drained and rinsed
- 1 tbsp olive oil
- Salt and pepper to taste
- 1/4 tsp cumin

Instructions

1. Over a medium-low heat, warm up the oil of olives in a big pan or steamer basket. Put in the onion and cook for about 5 minutes, until it gets soft.
2. Put in the garlic and cook for one more minute, until it smells good.
3. Add the turmeric, cumin, chili powder, and curry paste, and mix them in. Let the spices bloom for 30 seconds while you cook.
4. After you add the chickpeas, cook for two to three minutes, stirring every now and then.
5. Add the spinach pieces and cook until they wilt.
6. Whisk the eggs and milk together in a different bowl.
7. Add the egg mix to the chickpeas and vegetables in the pan or steamer basket.
8. For about 5 to 7 minutes, stir the mixture every now and then until the eggs are set and everything is hot. Add pepper and salt to taste.
9. Serve hot with naan bread that has been warmed up and chopped cilantro on top.

9. STEAMED YOGURT AND GRANOLA MUFFINS

Prep Time: 15 minutes Cook Time: 15-20 minutes

Total Time: 30-35 minutes

Servings: 12-14 muffins

Ingredients

- 1/2 cup of granola (your favorite flavor)
- 1 tsp vanilla extract
- 1/2 tsp baking soda
- 1 egg, lightly beaten
- 1/4 cup of honey
- 1/2 cup of plain Greek yogurt
- 1 tsp baking powder
- 1/3 cup of milk
- 1/4 tsp salt
- 1 1/2 cups of all-purpose flour
- Optional additions: 1/4 cup of chopped nuts, dried fruit, or chocolate chips

Instructions

1. Set your electric steamer to high temperature.
2. Add salt, flour, baking powder and baking soda to a large bowl and mix them together using a whisk.
3. Pour yogurt, milk, honey, egg, and vanilla extract into a different bowl and mix them together using a whisk.
4. Combine wet and dry components by adding them together and stirring just until everything is well mixed. Be careful not to mix too much.
5. Add the granola and any other ingredients you want and fold them in gently.
6. Utilize cooking spray to coat a silicone muffin pan or individual ramekins.
7. For each muffin cup of or ramekin, put an equal amount of batter in it.
8. Insert a toothpick into the middle of the pan and steam for 15 to 20 minutes, or until the toothpick comes out clean.
9. Before you serve the muffins, let them cool down a bit.

10. MINI STEAMED FRITTATAS WITH CHERRY TOMATOES

Prep Time: 15 minutes | Cook Time: 15-20 minutes

Total Time: 30-35 minutes

Servings: 12-14 mini frittatas

Ingredients

- 1/2 onion, finely chopped
- Salt and pepper to taste
- 1 pint cherry tomatoes, halved
- 1 tbsp olive oil
- Mini muffin pan greased with non-stick spray
- 1/4 cup of milk
- 4 eggs
- 1 clove garlic, minced
- 1/4 cup of grated Parmesan cheese
- 1/2 cup of fresh basil leaves, chopped (plus extra for garnish)

Instructions

1. Bring your electric steamer up to temperature.
2. Add eggs, milk, Parmesan cheese, salt, and pepper to a large bowl and mix them together using a whisk.
3. Set a skillet over moderate heat and add the olive oil. The onion will soften after about 5 minutes of cooking.
4. Continue cooking for one more minute after adding the garlic until it smells good.
5. Throw in the cherry tomatoes as well and cook for two to three minutes, until they get a little soft. Take the pan off the heat and let it cool down a bit.
6. The onion, garlic, and tomato mixture should be carefully folded into the egg mixture.
7. Incorporate the chopped basil leaves.
8. Equally fill each muffin cup of with the egg mixture.
9. Scramble the muffin pan in the steamer basket for 15 to 20 minutes, or until the frittata tops are golden brown and the eggs are set.
10. A little cooling time is needed before serving the mini frittatas.
11. Optional: Add more fresh basil leaves as a garnish.

11. STEAMED APPLE CRUMBLE WITH GREEK YOGURT

Prep Time: 15 minutes | Cook Time: 15-20 minutes

Total Time: 30-35 minutes

Servings: 4-6

Ingredients

For the Apples:

- 3-4 apples (tart varieties like Granny Smith work best)
- 1/4 cup of brown sugar
- 1 tsp ground cinnamon
- 1 tbsp lemon juice
- 1/4 tsp ground ginger (optional)
- Pinch of nutmeg (optional)

For the Crumble:

- 1/4 tsp ground cinnamon
- 2 tbsp cold unsalted butter, cubed
- 1/4 cup of brown sugar
- Pinch of salt
- 1/4 cup of all-purpose flour
- 1/4 cup of chopped walnuts or pecans
- 1/2 cup of rolled oats (quick or old-fashioned)

For Serving:

- 1 cup of plain Greek yogurt
- Fresh mint leaves (optional)
- Honey or maple syrup (optional)

Instructions

1. Get your electric steamer ready to go.
2. Just peel, core, and slice the apples very thinly. Combine them with brown sugar, cinnamon, ginger (if using), nutmeg, and lemon juice.
3. Oats, nuts, brown sugar, flour, cinnamon, and salt should all be mixed together in a bowl. With your fingers or a pastry cutter, cut the butter into the dry ingredients until you get crumbles about the size of peas.
4. Place an equal number of apples in each ramekin or small baking dish that can go in the oven. Really make sure to cover all of the apples with the crumble topping.
5. In the steamer basket, put the ramekins or baking dishes. Steam for 15 to 20 minutes, or until the apples are mushy and the crumble topping is golden brown and crunchy.
6. Using bowls, split the steamed apple crumble between them. Add some Greek yogurt to the top of each serving and, if you want, drizzle with honey or maple syrup. For an extra touch, add fresh mint leaves.

12. MANGO AND COCONUT STEAMED RICE PUDDING

Prep Time: 10 minutes | Cook Time: 20-25 minutes

Total Time: 30-35 minutes

Servings: 4-6

Ingredients

- 1/2 cup of cooked white rice (medium or long-grain)
- 1/4 cup of sugar
- 1 ripe mango, peeled and diced
- 1/4 tsp salt
- 1/2 cup of milk (dairy or non-dairy)
- 1/4 tsp freshly grated nutmeg
- 1 1/4 cups of full-fat coconut milk
- 1/2 tsp vanilla extract

Instructions

1. Get your electric steamer ready to go.
2. To make the pudding, mix cooked rice, milk, sugar, salt, nutmeg, and vanilla extract in a large bowl with a whisk. Fold the diced mango in slowly.
3. Spread the batter out evenly in ramekins or small baking dishes that can go in the oven.
4. In the steamer basket, put the ramekins or baking dishes. Cook for 20 to 25 minutes, or until the rice pudding is set and warm all the way through.
5. Let the pudding cool down a bit before you serve it.

13. VEGETABLE FRITTERS WITH AVOCADO SALSA

Prep Time: 20 minutes | Cook Time: 15-20 minutes

Total Time: 35-40 minutes

Servings: 4-6

Ingredients

For the Fritters:

- 1/4 cup of chopped fresh cilantro
- 1 cup of grated zucchini (squeeze out excess moisture)
- 1/2 cup of shredded carrots
- 1/2 cup of grated sweet potato
- 1/4 cup of all-purpose flour
- Salt and pepper to taste
- 1/4 tsp cumin
- 1/4 cup of cornmeal
- 1/4 cup of chopped yellow bell pepper
- 1 egg, beaten
- 1/4 cup of chopped red onion
- 1/4 tsp chili powder
- 1/4 tsp smoked paprika (optional)

For the Avocado Salsa:

- Salt and pepper to taste
- 1/4 tsp chili powder
- 1/4 cup of chopped red onion
- 1/4 cup of chopped fresh cilantro
- 1 ripe avocado, diced
- 1/2 cup of chopped ripe tomato
- 1 lime, juiced

Optional Garnishes:

- Sour cream
- Hot sauce
- Chopped fresh herbs like parsley or chives

Instructions

Warm up your electric steamer.

1. For the fritters, grate the zucchini, sweet potato, carrots, red onion, yellow bell pepper, and cilantro into a large bowl. Add pepper and salt. After 5 minutes, use a clean kitchen towel to squeeze out any extra water.
2. Add the cornmeal, cumin, chili powder, paprika (if using), and salt to a different bowl and mix them together using a whisk.
3. Mix the wet and dry components together until they are just mixed. Do not mix too much.
4. Add the beaten egg and combine it in.
5. Set a nonstick pan over medium heat. If your steamer basket is big enough to hold all the fritters, you can skip this step. A tbsp can be used to make small fritters. Carefully place them in the hot pan. It should be cooked for two to three minutes on each side, or until it turns golden brown and crispy.
6. You could also put the batter in muffin cups or ramekins that have been greased and put them in the steamer basket. Steam for 15 to 20 minutes, or until done and firm to the touch.
7. Dice the tomato, red onion, cilantro, lime juice, chili powder, and salt and put them in a bowl. Use a fork to lightly mix the avocado to make a chunky salsa. Add pepper to taste.
8. Put the vegetable fritters on a plate and add lots of avocado salsa on top of them. You can add sour cream, herbs, or hot sauce as a garnish if you want to.

14. STEAMED SAUSAGE AND SWEET POTATO

Prep Time: 20 minutes | Cook Time: 15-20 minutes

Total Time: 35-40 minutes

Servings: 2-3

Ingredients

- 1/4 tsp smoked paprika
- Salt and pepper to taste
- 1/4 red onion, chopped
- 1/4 cup of chopped fresh chives
- 2 eggs
- 1/2 pound breakfast sausage links (links or patties)
- 1 clove garlic, minced
- 1/4 tsp ground cumin
- 1 large sweet potato, peeled and cubed
- 1/2 bell pepper (any color), chopped
- Optional toppings: Chopped avocado, sour cream, hot sauce, fresh herbs

Instructions

1. Warm up your electric steamer.
2. Take the links out of their casings and crumble the sausage into a large bowl. Break up or chop patties into small pieces that are easy to eat.
3. Put the sweet potato cubes in a different bowl and add a little water. Put the bowl in the microwave on high for two to three minutes, or until the food gets a little softer. In the steamer, this step helps them cook faster.
4. The sweet potato should be soft. Add the bell pepper, red onion, salt, garlic, chives, cumin, paprika, and pepper to the bowl with the sausage. Combine well by mixing.
5. Spread the mixture out evenly in ramekins or small baking dishes that can go in the oven. Put the baking dishes or ramekins in the basket of a steamer and steam for 15 to 20 minutes, or until the sweet the potatoes are soft and warm all the way through.
6. Get your eggs ready while the hash is steaming. You can choose to fry them sunny side up, poach them, or scramble them.
7. Put the steamed hash on a plate and add a cooked egg on top of it. Add your favorite toppings, like chopped avocado, sour cream, hot sauce, or fresh herbs, to make it taste and feel better.

15. POACHED EGGS ON STEAMED SPINACH

Prep Time: 10 minutes Cook Time: 15 minutes

Total Time: 25 minutes

Servings: 2

Ingredients

- 2 cups of fresh spinach
- 1 clove garlic, minced (optional)
- 1 tbsp white vinegar
- 2 slices smoked salmon
- Salt and pepper to taste
- 2 eggs
- 1 tbsp olive oil
- Optional toppings: Chopped fresh chives, dill, or parsley, toasted bagel slices, hollandaise sauce

Instructions

1. Put a few inches of water in a big pot and bring it to a slight boil. Over the pot, put a steamer basket or colander.
2. Salt and pepper the spinach before putting it in the steamer basket. Cover and steam for two to three minutes, or until the leaves are soft and bright green. Take it out of the steamer and set it aside.
3. In a tiny skillet over medium heat, heat the olive oil if you want to use it. Put in the minced garlic and cook for one minute, until the garlic smells good.
4. Put about three inches of water in a saucepan and heat it over low heat. Put the vinegar in. Put a different egg into a separate small bowl or ramekin. Use a spoon to stir the water slowly to make a small whirlpool.
5. Put one egg at a time into the water that is just starting to boil, close to the middle of the whirlpool. Leave it to cook for three to four minutes, or until the egg whites are set but the yolks are still warm. Take the eggs out of the water with a slotted spoon and drain any extra water.
6. Put some steamed spinach on each of two plates. On top of the spinach, put the smoked salmon. Put a poached egg on each plate carefully. If you wish, you can add additional pepper and salt to taste.
7. Add chopped fresh herbs like chives, dill, or parsley as a garnish to make the dish taste even better. You can make brunch even more decadent by serving it with toasted bagel slices or hollandaise sauce.

16. CINNAMON SPICED STEAMED OATMEAL

Prep Time: 5 minutes | Cook Time: 15-20 minutes

Total Time: 20-25 minutes

Servings: 1-2

Ingredients

- 1 tbsp chopped nuts (pecans, walnuts, almonds, etc.)
- 1 tbsp honey (adjust to your sweetness preference)
- 1/4 tsp ground cinnamon
- 1 cup of water or milk (dairy or non-dairy)
- 1/2 cup of rolled oats (old-fashioned or quick)
- Pinch of salt
- Optional toppings: Fresh fruit, shredded coconut, maple syrup, chia seeds

Instructions

1. Warm up your electric steamer.
2. Put rolled oats, water or milk, cinnamon, and salt in a small bowl or ramekin. Mix well.
3. In a steamer basket, put the bowl or ramekin. Steam for 15 to 20 minutes, or until the oats are soft and cooked all the way through. While it's steaming, stir it every so often.
4. Add the chopped nuts to a air-dry pan and heat it over medium-low heat. Toast them until they turn golden brown and smell good. Put away.
5. Move the oatmeal to a bowl for serving after it's done cooking. Add the honey and toasted nuts and mix them in.
6. Have fun warm! Put your favorite things on top, like chia seeds, fresh fruit, shredded coconut, maple syrup, or shredded coconut, to make it taste and feel better.

17. MINI STEAMED BREAKFAST BURRITOS

Prep Time: 15 minutes | Cook Time: 15-20 minutes

Total Time: 30-35 minutes

Servings: 6-8 mini burritos

Ingredients

For the Filling:

- 1/4 tsp chili powder
- 1/2 tsp ground cumin
- 1 (15 ounce) can black beans, drained and rinsed
- 1/4 cup of shredded cheddar cheese
- 1/2 cup of diced bell pepper
- 1/4 cup of chopped red onion
- 1 clove garlic, minced
- Pinch of salt and pepper
- 1/4 cup of crumbled Cotija cheese (optional)

For the Wraps:

- 6-8 small (6-inch) tortillas (flour or corn)

Optional Toppings:

- Salsa
- Sour cream
- Hot sauce
- Chopped avocado

Instructions

1. Warm up one tbsp of olive oil in a medium-sized pan over medium-low heat. It will take 5 minutes for the bell pepper and red onion to get soft after you add them.
2. After you add the garlic, cumin, and chili powder, cook for one more minute or until the food smells good.
3. Add the black beans that have been drained and season with salt and pepper. Heat it up for three to four minutes, until it's all warm.
4. Take it off the heat and add the torn cheddar cheese. Allow to cool a bit.
5. Put the burritos together: Place the tortilla flat on a clean surface. In the middle, put a spoonful of the black bean mix. If you're using it, sprinkle with Cotija cheese.
6. First, fold the bottom of the tortilla up over the filling. Then, fold the sides in toward the center. Make a burrito by rolling it up tight.
7. To steam the burritos, put them in a single layer in the basket of your steamer. Set a pot on low heat and add a few inches of water. Cover the pot and put the steamer basket on top of it. Steam for 15 to 20 minutes, or until everything is hot.
8. Serve: Your mini breakfast burritos are ready to eat at this point. Put your favorite things on top, like salsa, sour cream, avocado, or hot sauce.

18. STRAWBERRY AND RICOTTA STEAMED CREPES

Prep Time: 15 minutes | Cook Time: 15-20 minutes

Total Time: 30-35 minutes

Servings: 4-6 crepes

Ingredients

For the Crepes:

- 1 tbsp melted butter
- 1 cup of all-purpose flour
- 1/4 cup of water
- 2 eggs
- 1 tbsp sugar
- 1 cup of milk (dairy or non-dairy)
- Pinch of salt

For the Filling:

- 2 tbsp honey
- 1 cup of fresh strawberries, sliced
- 1/2 cup of ricotta cheese
- Fresh mint leaves (optional)
- 1/4 tsp vanilla extract

Instructions

1. Combine flour, eggs, milk, water, sugar, and salt in a large bowl. Use a blender to blend the ingredients together until the good is smooth and free of lumps.
2. Pour in the warm butter and mix it in with a whisk. Take 15 minutes to let the batter rest. Get your electric steamer ready to go.
3. Put the Filling together: Sliced strawberries, ricotta cheese, honey, and vanilla extract should all be mixed together in a bowl. Make sure not to crush the strawberries as you mix the ingredients together.
4. Create the crepes: If your steamer basket is big enough to hold all the crepes, you can skip this step and just heat a nonstick pan over medium hot heat. Measure out or use a ladle to pour with 1/4 cup of dough into the pan. It will help the batter spread out if you swirl the pan. For one to two minutes, or until the edges begin to brown and the center is set, it's done.
5. You could also put about 1/4 cup of batter in muffin cups or ramekins that have been greased and put them in the steamer basket. After two to three minutes of steaming, the food is done.
6. Assemble a crepe and set it on a plate. Put a small amount of the ricotta-strawberry filling in the middle. If you'd rather, you can fold the crepe in half or roll it up.
7. Do steps 5 through 7 again with the rest of the filling and batter.
8. Serve: If you want, drizzle with more honey or a little balsamic glaze. Add some fresh mint leaves on top to make it taste even better.

19. TROPICAL SMOOTHIE BOWL WITH STEAMED QUINOA

Prep Time: 10 minutes | Cook Time: 7 minutes

Total Time: 17 minutes

Servings: 1 bowl

Ingredients

For the Smoothie:

- 1/4 cup of unsweetened almond milk (or milk of your choice)
- 1 frozen banana
- Pinch of vanilla extract
- 1/2 cup of frozen mango chunks
- 1/4 cup of plain Greek yogurt (optional, for extra protein)
- 1/4 cup of frozen pineapple chunks
- 1/2 tsp ground ginger (optional, for a spicy kick)

For the Steamed Quinoa:

- 1/4 cup of rinsed quinoa
- 1/2 cup of water

For the Fruit Topping:

- 1/2 cup of fresh mango, diced
- 1/4 cup of fresh pineapple, diced
- 1/4 cup of fresh blueberries
- 1/4 cup of fresh raspberries
- 1 tbsp shredded coconut (optional)
- Fresh mint leaves (optional, for a refreshing touch)

Instructions

1. Put the frozen fruits in a bowl and let them sit at room temperature for a few minutes while you get the quinoa ready. In this way, they will blend better.
2. Put water in your electric steamer basket and then turn it down to a low heat. Rinse the quinoa and put it in a ramekin or a small dish that can go in the oven. Put just enough water in the dish or ramekin to cover the quinoa. Cover the ramekin and put it in the steamer basket. Steam the quinoa for 15 to 20 minutes, or until it's fluffy and fully cooked.
3. Putting everything into a blender and blending it until it's smooth and creamy. If you need to, add more almond milk (or any other milk you like) to get the consistency you want.
4. A pretty bowl should be used to hold the smoothie. Put the fluffy quinoa on top, then the colorful diced pineapple, mango, blueberries, and raspberries. If you wish, you can add new mint leaves and shredded coconut on top.
5. Get ready for a bright tropical escape in a bowl! Enjoy every spoonful of the smooth smoothie, the crunchy quinoa, and the burst of fresh fruit flavors.

20. STEAMED BANANA AND OATMEAL PANCAKES

Prep Time: 10 minutes | Cook Time: 15-20 minutes

Total Time: 25-30 minutes

Servings: 6-8 pancakes

Ingredients

For the Pancakes:

- 1 tsp baking powder
- 1/2 cup of whole wheat flour
- 1 egg, beaten
- 1 ripe banana, mashed
- 1/2 cup of rolled oats
- 1 tsp vanilla extract
- 1 cup of milk (dairy or non-dairy)
- 1/4 tsp salt

For the Maple Pecans:

- 1/4 tsp ground cinnamon
- 2 tbsp maple syrup
- 1/4 cup of chopped pecans

Optional Toppings:

- Yogurt
- Fresh fruit (berries, bananas, etc.)
- Honey or maple syrup
- Whipped cream (optional)

Instructions

1. In a large bowl, use a whisk to mix the rolled oats, flour, baking powder, and salt together.
2. Utilize a fork to mash the banana in a different bowl. While whisking, add the milk, egg, and vanilla extract.
3. Combine the dry and wet ingredients by slowly stirring them together. Not too much mixing.
4. Lightly grease the basket of your electric steamer. You can oil-dipped bristles or cooking spray. Another option is to grease ramekins or other small oven-safe dishes and put them in the steamer basket.
5. Put about 1/4 cup of pancake batter into the ramekins or steamer basket. Put about half of the mixture into each ramekin. The pancakes should be fluffy and cooked all the way through after 10 to 15 minutes of steaming in a pot of water that is just simmering.
6. Warm the cinnamon and maple syrup in a small pan over medium-low heat while the pancakes are cooking. While stirring constantly for two to three minutes, add the pecans and cook until they are coated and toasted.
7. Put the steamed pancakes on plates and garnish them with the pecans. For example, you could put on fresh fruit, yogurt, honey or maple syrup, and whipped cream.

COMFORT FOOD

21. FLUFFY STEAMED MAC AND CHEESE

Prep Time: 10 minutes | Cook Time: 20-25 minutes

Total Time: 30-35 minutes

Servings: 4-6

Ingredients

For the Creamy Cheese Sauce:

- 1/2 tsp salt
- 2 cups of milk (dairy or non-dairy)
- 8 ounces shredded cheddar cheese (divided)
- 1/4 tsp black pepper
- 4 ounces shredded mozzarella cheese
- 2 tbsp all-purpose flour
- 2 tbsp butter
- 1/4 tsp paprika (optional)

For the Macaroni:

- 1/4 cup of grated Parmesan cheese
- 8 ounces elbow macaroni

Instructions

1. To make the cheese sauce, warm the butter over medium-low heat in a small saucepan. Add the flour and stir it in. Cook for one minute, until the food turns golden brown.
2. Carefully whisk in the milk, making sure there are no lumps. Turn the heat up to medium-high and let it simmer.
3. Add the paprika, pepper, salt and mix them in. Turn down the heat and let it simmer for 5 minutes, until it gets thick.
4. Take the pan off the heat and add 6 ounces of cheddar cheese and the mozzarella cheese. Mix the cheeses in until they melt and become creamy. Put away.
5. Get the macaroni ready: Put water in your electric steamer basket and then turn it down to a low heat. Put the macaroni in a ramekin or a small dish that can go in the oven. Just cover the pasta with water in the ramekin. Cover the ramekin and put it in the steamer basket. This will cook the pasta until it is just right.
6. Combine and Cheese Up: Once the macaroni is done, drain it and add it right away to the saucepan with the cheese sauce. Mix everything together slowly.
7. To put it all together and serve, divide the macaroni and cheese mixture among bowls. Add the last 2 ounces of cheddar cheese that has been shredded and the grated Parmesan cheese to the top of each serving.

22. STEAMED CHICKEN POT PIE WITH PUFF PASTRY CRUST

Prep Time: 15 minutes | Cook Time: 25-30 minutes

Total Time: 40-45 minutes

Servings: 4-6

Ingredients

For the Filling:

- 1 carrot, chopped
- 1 small onion, chopped
- 2 cups of cooked chicken, shredded
- 1/4 tsp dried thyme
- Salt and pepper to taste
- 1/2 cup of frozen corn
- 1 celery stalk, chopped
- 1 cup of frozen peas
- 1 tbsp olive oil
- 1/2 cup of chicken broth
- 1/4 cup of milk (dairy or non-dairy)
- 2 cloves garlic, minced

For the Puff Pastry Crust:

- 1 egg, beaten (for egg wash)
- 1 sheet frozen puff pastry, thawed
- Optional toppings: fresh herbs, sesame seeds, black pepper

Instructions

1. First, melt the butter in a small saucepan over medium-low heat. This will help you make the cheese sauce. As you whisk, slowly add the flour. Let it cook for one minute or until it turns golden brown.
2. As you slowly add the milk, make sure there are no lumps. Turn up the heat to medium-high and let it simmer.
3. Add the pepper, salt, and paprika (if using) and mix well. Turn down the heat to low and let it simmer for 5 minutes, until it gets thick.
4. Get the pan off the heat and add 6 ounces of cheddar cheese and the mozzarella cheese. Mix the cheeses in until they melt and become creamy. Save for later.
5. Get the pasta ready: Turn on your electric steamer and add water to the basket. In a ramekin or other small oven-safe dish, put the macaroni. Simply fill the ramekin with water until it just covers the pasta. Just put the ramekin in the steamer basket and cover it. Let the pasta steam for 10 to 15 minutes, or until it is just barely done.
6. Mix it up: Once the macaroni is done, drain it and add it right away to the saucepan with the cheese sauce. Mix slowly by stirring.
7. Put it all together and serve by dividing the macaroni and cheese mixture among bowls. Garnish each serving with the last two ounces of shredded cheddar cheese and the grated Parmesan cheese.

23. SAVORY STEAMED MEATLOAF WITH GLAZED CARROTS

Prep Time: 15 minutes | Cook Time: 35-40 minutes

Total Time: 50-55 minutes

Servings: 4-6

Ingredients

For the Meatloaf:

- 1 egg, beaten
- 1/2 cup of breadcrumbs
- Salt and pepper to taste
- 1 pound ground beef or turkey (leanest you can find)
- 1/4 tsp dried thyme
- 1/4 cup of grated onion
- 1/2 tsp garlic powder
- 1 tbsp Dijon mustard
- 1 tbsp ketchup
- 1/4 cup of chopped fresh parsley

For the Glazed Carrots:

- 1/4 cup of honey
- 1 tsp olive oil
- 2 tbsp Dijon mustard
- 1 pound baby carrots, trimmed and halved
- 1/4 tsp fresh rosemary, chopped (optional)

Instructions

1. Bring water in your steamer basket to a simmer to heat it up. Mix all the meatloaf ingredients together: Grate the onion, add the parsley, salt, egg, ketchup, Dijon mustard, garlic powder, thyme, and pepper to a large bowl. Then mix the meat mixture well.
2. Cut the meatloaf into: Put the meat mixture on a plate or shallow baking dish that fits inside your steamer basket and shape it into a loaf shape.
3. Make the meatloaf steamy: Cover the steamer basket and put the baking dish with the meatloaf inside it. Steam the meatloaf for 35 to 40 minutes or until it reaches 160°F on the inside. Though the meatloaf is cooking: Get the carrots ready to be glazed. Add the honey, Dijon mustard, olive oil, and rosemary (if using) to a small bowl and mix them together using a whisk.
4. Put the carrots in: After 20 minutes of steaming, carefully open the steamer and put the carrots around the meatloaf. Add the honey-mustard glaze to the carrots and spread it out. Put the lid on top and keep steaming for another 15 to 20 minutes.
5. Take a break and serve: Take the carrots and meatloaf out of the steamer and let them rest for 5 minutes. Then you can cut them up and serve them. This keeps the meatloaf from falling apart by letting the juices move around.
6. Have fun! For a healthy and filling meal, cut the meatloaf into pieces and serve them with the glazed carrots.

24. STICKY HONEY GARLIC SALMON WITH BROCCOLI

Prep Time: 10 minutes | Cook Time: 15-20 minutes

Total Time: 25-30 minutes

Servings: 2-3

Ingredients

For the Honey Garlic Salmon:

- 2 salmon fillets (4-6 ounce each), skin-on or skinless
- 1 tbsp honey
- 1 tsp minced garlic
- 1 tbsp rice vinegar
- 1 tbsp soy sauce
- 1/4 tsp black pepper
- 1 tbsp brown sugar
- 1/2 tsp ground ginger
- 1 tbsp toasted sesame seeds (optional)

For the Steamed Broccoli:

- 1 head broccoli, cut into florets

Instructions

1. To get the salmon ready, mix the soy sauce, brown sugar, honey, rice vinegar, garlic, ginger, and black pepper in a non-deep bowl. Put the salmon fillets in the sauce and flip them over once halfway through the 10 minutes.
2. Bring water to a simmer in your electric steamer basket to heat it up.
3. To steam broccoli, put the florets in the steamer basket and cover it. Steam for three to five minutes, or until the potatoes are just barely crisp. Put the broccoli that has been steamed on a plate and set it aside.
4. Place the salmon fillets in the steamer basket with the broccoli. If using skin-on, put the salmon fillets skin-side up. For 10 to 15 minutes, or until the salmon is opaque and flaky when pierced with a fork, cover and steam.
5. As the salmon is steaming, mix 1 tbsp of the marinade with 1 tbsp of water in a small saucepan. You can also toast the salmon while it's cooking. Over medium-low heat, bring to a boil. Brush the glaze over the tops of the salmon fillets once it's done cooking. For an extra nutty taste, if you want to, sprinkle with toasted sesame seeds.
6. Put it all together and serve. Put the glazed salmon fillets on top of the steamed broccoli on a plate. If there is any glaze left in the pan, drizzle it on top (optional). Have fun with your tasty and healthy Electric Steamer Sticky Honey Garlic Salmon with Broccoli!

25. SPICY KOREAN BEEF BULGOGI BOWL WITH BROWN RICE

Prep Time: 15 minutes | Cook Time: 25-30 minutes

Total Time: 40-45 minutes

Servings: 2-3 generous bowls

Ingredients

For the Spicy Korean Beef Bulgogi:

- 2 tbsp brown sugar
- 1/4 cup of soy sauce
- 1 tbsp rice vinegar
- 1 pound flank steak or sirloin steak, thinly sliced against the grain
- 2 tbsp gochujang (Korean chili paste)
- 1/4 tsp black pepper
- 1/2 tsp sesame oil
- 1 tbsp minced garlic
- 1 tsp grated ginger
- 1 tbsp honey
- Pinch of red pepper flakes (optional, for extra spice)

For the Brown Rice:

- 1 1/2 cups of water
- 1 cup of brown rice

For the Bowl Toppings:

- 2 cups of mixed greens (spinach, romaine, etc.)
- 1/4 cup of julienned carrots
- 1/2 cup of kimchi, chopped
- Sesame seeds, to garnish
- 1/4 cup of sliced cucumber
- 1/4 cup of chopped scallions
- Optional additional toppings: sliced avocado, fried egg, toasted seaweed snacks

Instructions

1. To prepare the beef, mix the soy sauce, black pepper, sesame oil, brown sugar, rice vinegar, gochujang, ginger, honey, garlic and red pepper flakes (if using) in a large bowl. Toss the sliced beef in the sauce to coat it well. Cover and let it sit for at least 30 minutes. For better flavor, let it sit overnight.
2. Make the brown rice: Rinse the brown rice and put it in a pot or rice cooker with water. Slowly raise the heat, cover, and let it cook for 20 to 25 minutes, or until the rice is fluffy and fully cooked.
3. Optional: Steam the Beef: If you want to, heat up your electric steamer basket with water and bring it to a simmer while the rice cooks. Lay the beef that has been marinated out in a single layer in the steamer basket. Then, cover it. Let it steam for 10 to 15 minutes, or until it's fully cooked. This method makes a dish that is both healthy and juicy.
4. As an alternative, If you'd rather pan-fry the beef, heat a large skillet over medium-high flames. Put a little oil on the pan and cook the beef in batches for three to four minutes on each side, or until it's browned and done.
5. Put the Bowls Together: Put the cooked brown rice into bowls. Add the scallions, kimchi, julienned carrots, and cucumber on top of the mixed greens. Place the cooked beef on top of the other ingredients.
6. Add sesame seeds and enjoy! You can add your favorite toppings, like fried eggs, sliced avocado, or toasted seaweed snacks, if you want to add more flavor and texture.

26. STEAMED CHICKEN AND DUMPLINGS

Prep Time: 15 minutes | Cook Time: 20-25 minutes

Total Time: 35-40 minutes

Servings: 4-6

Ingredients:

For the Herb Broth:

- 1 sprig fresh thyme
- 1/2 tsp dried parsley
- 1 carrot, thinly sliced
- 1 bay leaf
- 2 cloves garlic, minced
- 1 onion, chopped
- 4 cups of chicken broth (low-sodium preferred)
- 2 stalks celery, thinly sliced
- Salt and pepper to taste

For the Chicken and Dumplings:

- 1 tbsp chopped fresh parsley
- 1/4 tsp salt
- 1/2 cup of all-purpose flour
- 1/4 cup of rolled oats
- 1 skinless, boneless chicken breast, cooked and shredded
- 1/4 tsp baking powder
- 1/4 cup of milk (dairy or non-dairy)

Instructions

1. Put the chicken broth, celery, carrot, onion, garlic, thyme sprig, bay leaf, and parsley in a large pot. This will make the herb broth. Bring it to a boil, then turn down the heat and let it cook for 15 minutes. This will let the flavors mix. Add pepper and salt to taste.
2. Get the dumpling dough ready: In a medium-sized bowl, oats, baking powder, use a whisk to mix the flour, and salt. Add the milk and chopped parsley and mix well until a soft dough forms. If you need to, add more milk until the mixture is thick enough to work with.
3. To put the dumplings together, roll out the dough to about 1/4-inch thickness on a lightly floured surface. Use a cookie cutter or a glass to make circles. Put a scoop of chicken shreds in the middle of each circle.
4. To steam the dumplings, grease a steamer basket or some small dishes that can go in the oven. Put the dumplings in a way that gives them room to grow. Cover the steamer basket and put it over the simmering broth. Steam for 10 to 15 minutes, or until the dumplings are fluffy and cooked all the way through.
5. Finish: Take out the steamer basket and throw away the bay leaf and thyme sprig. Add the cooked dumplings to the hot herb broth and stir them in slowly. Add fresh parsley or chives as a garnish (optional) and serve right away.

27. CLASSIC AMERICAN CHEESEBURGERS

Prep Time: 10 minutes | Cook Time: 15-20 minutes

Total Time: 25-30 minutes

Servings: 4

Ingredients:

For the Burgers:

- 1/4 tsp garlic powder
- 1 pound ground beef (leanest you can find)
- 1/2 tsp salt
- 1/4 tsp black pepper
- 1/4 tsp onion powder
- Optional: 1 tbsp ketchup or Dijon mustard for added moisture

For the Toppings:

- 4 lettuce leaves
- 4 slices cheddar cheese
- 4 tomato slices
- 4 onion slices
- 4 hamburger buns (toasted, optional)
- Ketchup, mustard, mayonnaise, pickles, and any other desired toppings

Instructions

1. Bring water to a simmer in your electric steamer basket to heat it up.
2. Put the ground beef, salt, pepper, garlic powder, onion powder, and ketchup or mustard (if using) in a large bowl and mix them together slowly. Mix just until everything is combined; don't work the meat too much.
3. Scoop out four equal amounts of the meat mixture and shape them into patties that are just a bit bigger than the buns' diameter.
4. Cover the steamer basket and put the patties in it. Steam for 15 to 20 minutes, or until the meat reaches 160°F for medium-well doneness. Set the timer for the level of doneness you want.
5. While the burgers are cooking, make the buns however you like. They can be toasted in the oven, toaster, or grill.
6. Put a burger patty that has been steamed on each bun. Put your favorite cheeseburger toppings on top, like tomato, onion, lettuce, ketchup, mustard, mayonnaise, pickles, and so on. Get creative, and enjoy your American cheeseburger that is lighter and better for you.

28. STEAMED SALMON AND ASPARAGUS

Prep Time: 10 minutes | Cook Time: 12-15 minutes

Total Time: 22-25 minutes

Servings: 2

Ingredients

For the Salmon and Asparagus:

- 2 salmon fillets (4-6 ounce each), skin-on or skinless
- 1/4 cup of water
- 1 bunch asparagus, trimmed

For the Lemon Butter Sauce:

- 2 tbsp lemon juice
- Pinch of black pepper
- 4 tbsp butter, softened
- 1/4 tsp salt
- 1/2 tsp grated lemon zest

Instructions

1. Prepare the salmon and asparagus. If you're using salmon with the skin still on, pat it dry and use a sharp knife to make diagonal cuts in the skin. Leave the tips of the asparagus whole when you trim them.
2. How to make the lemon butter sauce: Mix the softened butter, salt, lemon juice, lemon zest, and pepper in a small bowl with a whisk until the mixture is smooth and creamy.
3. Bring water to a simmer in your electric steamer basket to heat it up.
4. Bring the salmon and asparagus to a boil: For skin-on salmon, put the fillets in the steamer basket with the skin side facing up. Place the asparagus around the salmon. Put the 1/4 cup of water in the basket's bottom. Put the lid on top and steam for 12 to 15 minutes, or until the asparagus is soft but crisp and the salmon is opaque.
5. Serve and Have Fun: Place the asparagus and salmon on plates. Add a lot of the lemon butter sauce to each serving. If you wish, you can add fresh plants like dill or parsley as a garnish. Have a nice time with your lemon butter steamed salmon and asparagus.

29. VEGETABLE LASAGNA WITH RICOTTA AND SPINACH

Prep Time: 20 minutes | Cook Time: 40-45 minutes

Total Time: 60-65 minutes

Servings: 4-6

Ingredients

For the Roasted Vegetables:

- 1 bell pepper (your choice of color), thinly sliced
- 1 zucchini, thinly sliced
- 1 tbsp olive oil
- 1 red onion, thinly sliced
- 1/2 tsp salt
- 1 yellow squash, thinly sliced
- 1/4 tsp black pepper

For the Ricotta and Spinach Filling:

- 1/2 cup of grated Parmesan cheese
- 1/4 tsp salt
- 15 ounce ricotta cheese (whole or part-skim)
- 1/4 cup of chopped fresh parsley
- Pinch of black pepper
- 1 cup of chopped fresh spinach

For the Tomato Sauce (Optional):

- 1 clove garlic, minced
- Pinch of black pepper
- 1/2 tsp dried oregano
- 1/4 tsp salt
- 1 (28-ounce) can crushed tomatoes
- 1 tbsp olive oil

For the Assembly:

- 12 no-boil lasagna noodles
- 1/2 cup of shredded mozzarella cheese

Instructions

1. Bring water to a simmer in your electric steamer basket to heat it up.
2. You can choose to roast the vegetables. Warm the oven up to 200°C (400°F). Add the bell pepper, red onion, zucchini, and yellow squash to a bowl. Put in the pepper, salt, and olive oil. Place them on a baking sheet and roast them for 15 to 20 minutes, or until they are hot and crispy. If you want the vegetables to be softer, steam them in the steamer basket for 5 to 7 minutes instead of roasting them.
3. Fill the shells with ricotta and spinach. Chop the spinach and put it in a large bowl. Add the ricotta cheese, Parmesan cheese, parsley, salt, and pepper. Mix well until everything is smooth and creamy.
4. If you want to, make the tomato sauce: If you are going to use the olive oil, warm it up a little in a small pot over medium-low heat. After you add the garlic, cook for 30 seconds or until it smells good. Add the olives, oregano, salt, and pepper, and mix them in. Slowly bring to a boil. Then cook for 5 minutes, stirring every now and then.
5. Put together the lasagna: Use a baking dish that fits inside your steamer basket and spread some tomato sauce on the bottom of it.
6. Put three lasagna noodles on top of it. Put some ricotta and spinach filling on top of the noodles. If you want, you can add roasted vegetables on top and sprinkle some mozzarella cheese on top. Do this again, ending with a layer of noodles, ricotta and spinach filling, and the rest of the mozzarella cheese.
7. Put the lasagna in the steamer: Put the baking dish in the steamer basket and cover it with foil. Steam the lasagna for 40 to 45 minutes, or until it's hot all the way through and bubbly.
8. Rest and Serve: Take the lasagna out of the steamer and let it sit for 10 minutes. Then cut it into pieces and serve. Enjoy your Electric Steamer Vegetable Lasagna with Ricotta and Spinach, which is light and tasty.

30. STEAMED CHICKEN AND VEGETABLE CURRY

Prep Time: 15 minutes | Cook Time: 25-30 minutes

Total Time: 40-45 minutes

Servings: 4

Ingredients

For the Steamed Chicken and Vegetables:

- 1 pound boneless, skinless chicken breast, cut into bite-sized pieces
- 1 clove garlic, minced
- 1/2 cup of bell pepper
- 1/4 cup of water
- 1 cup of broccoli florets
- 1/2 cup of chopped onion
- 1/2 tsp ground ginger

For the Curry Sauce:

- 1 tbsp curry powder
- 1/4 tsp turmeric
- 1 (14.5 ounce) can diced tomatoes,
- Pinch of cayenne pepper (optional)
- 1/2 cup of chopped fresh cilantro
- 1/2 tsp ground coriander
- 1 tsp ground cumin
- 1 tbsp vegetable oil
- 1/2 cup of coconut milk
- 1 tbsp tomato paste
- 1 tbsp honey or maple syrup

For Serving:

- 4 pieces naan bread (warmed)
- Lime wedges (optional)

Instructions

1. Bring the water in your electric steamer basket to a simmer to heat it up.
2. Put the vegetables and chicken in a steamer: Put the broccoli, onion, garlic, ginger, bell pepper, chicken, and water in a bowl. After coating, put in the steamer basket. Place the lid on top and steam for 15 to 20 minutes, or until the vegetables are soft but still crisp and the chicken is cooked through.
3. Get the curry sauce ready: While the vegetables and chicken are steaming, heat the oil in a large saucepan over medium-low heat. If you're using it, add the cayenne pepper, cumin, coriander, turmeric, and curry powder. To release the fragrant smell, cook for 30 seconds while stirring all the time.
4. Put in the rest of the sauce's ingredients: Combine the tomato paste, honey or maple syrup, coconut milk, diced tomatoes, and 1/2 cup of water. Bring it to a simmer, then cook for 5 minutes while stirring every now and then.
5. Gather and Serve: Add the vegetables and chicken that have been steamed to the saucepan with the curry sauce. Mix slowly to mix, and heat for one more minute. Serve right away with warm naan bread and chopped cilantro as a garnish. You can add a little acidity to your curry by squeezing wedges of lime over it.

31. FLUFFY WHITE STEAMED BUNS

Prep Time: 2 hours | Cook Time: 15 minutes

Total Time: 2 hours 15 minutes

Servings: 12-15 buns

Ingredients

For the Dough:

- 1/4 cup of granulated sugar
- 1 tbsp vegetable oil
- 1 1/4 cups of warm milk
- 1/2 tsp salt
- 3 cups of all-purpose flour
- 1 1/2 tsp active dry yeast

For Steaming:

- Parchment paper squares

Instructions

1. Add the dry items to the wet ones. Use a whisk to mix the yeast, sugar, salt, and flour in a large bowl. For the yeast to work, make a well in the middle of the dry ingredients. Combine the warm milk and vegetable oil. Allow the yeast to work for five minutes by letting it sit.
2. You can knead the dough for 7 to 10 minutes with your hands or a dough hook on a stand mixer, until it is smooth and springy. Knead the dough on a surface that has been lightly dusted with flour until it stops sticking. Do something with your hands.
3. First rise: Put the dough in a clean bowl that has been greased and turn it over once to coat it. If you put it somewhere warm for an hour, it should double in size. Place plastic wrap over it and leave it there. To make the buns, make the dough flat and knead it slowly for one minute. Split the dough into 12 to 15 equal pieces. For a fluffy result, roll each piece into a smooth ball that you can shape as tightly as you can.
4. Second rise: Leave enough space between the buns on the parchment paper squares so they can rise. Place a piece of plastic wrap over them loosely and let them rise for another 30 minutes. To heat up the steamer, put water in the basket of your electric steamer and bring it to a simmer. If you don't have a rack in your steamer, line it with a cabbage leaf or something else that can handle heat to keep the buns from sticking.
5. Prepare the buns for steaming by placing them on the steamer rack or cabbage leaf, leaving space between each one. Tent with a lid and steam for 15 minutes. It's important not to peek while the buns are steaming because it can stop them from rising properly. Let the buns cool down for 5 minutes before taking them out of the steamer to enjoy. Just put them on a wire structure to cool down all the way. Fill your fluffy white steamed buns with your favorite sweet or savory things, eat them by themselves, or dip them in soy sauce, sesame oil, or sweet and sour sauce.

32. CREAMY POLENTA WITH GRILLED VEGETABLES

Prep Time: 20 minutes | Cook Time: 40 minutes

Total Time: 60 minutes

Servings: 4-6

Ingredients

For the Creamy Polenta:

- 4 cups of water
- 1 cup (1/2 cup dry) polenta
- 1/2 tsp salt
- 1/4 tsp black pepper
- 2 tbsp butter
- 1/2 cup of grated Parmesan cheese

For the Grilled Vegetables:

- 1 red bell pepper, sliced
- 1 yellow bell pepper, sliced
- 1 zucchini, sliced
- 1 red onion, sliced
- 1 tbsp olive oil
- 1/2 tsp salt
- 1/4 tsp black pepper

For Serving (Optional):

- Fresh herbs like basil or parsley, chopped
- Additional Parmesan cheese

Instructions

1. Bring the water in your electric steamer basket to a simmer to heat it up.
2. Get the polenta ready by: Add the water, salt, and pepper to a saucepan and mix them together. Finally, add the polenta slowly while whisking the mixture. Lower the heat to low and let it simmer while stirring all the time for 20 to 25 minutes, or until it gets thick and creamy. After taking it off the heat, add the butter and Parmesan cheese and stir them in until they are fully mixed in.
3. Get the veggies ready: Cut the zucchini, bell pepper, and red onion into thin slices. Salt, pepper, and olive oil should be added to them.
4. Warm up the griddle: Set your grill pan on medium-high heat to get it hot. You could also use an outdoor grill.
5. For the vegetables, grill: To get the vegetables tender-crisp and nicely charred, grill them in groups for three to four minutes on each side.
6. Gather and serve: Place the smooth polenta on plates. Place grilled vegetables on top and, if you want, add more Parmesan cheese and fresh herbs. Electric Steamer Creamy Polenta with Grilled Vegetables and Parmesan is light and tasty.

33. STEAMED SHRIMP WONTONS

Prep Time: 20 minutes | Cook Time: 12-15 minutes

Total Time: 32-35 minutes

Servings: 4-6

Ingredients:

For the Wontons:

- 1/4 cup of chopped cilantro
- 1 tsp soy sauce
- 1 cup of all-purpose flour
- 1/2 cup of chopped green onions
- 12 large shrimp, peeled and deveined
- 1/2 tsp sesame oil
- 1/4 tsp salt
- 1 tbsp minced ginger
- Pinch of black pepper
- 1 tbsp vegetable oil
- 1/4 cup of cold water

For the Spicy Dipping Sauce:

- 1/4 cup of rice vinegar
- 1 tbsp sesame oil
- 1 tbsp sriracha or chili sauce (adjust to your spice preference)
- 1/4 cup of soy sauce
- 1 tsp minced garlic
- 1/2 tsp minced ginger
- Pinch of red pepper flakes (optional)
- Sesame seeds and chopped green onions, for garnish (optional)

Instructions:

1. Put the flour and salt in a large bowl and mix them together with a whisk. Add the cold water and oil slowly while mixing until a dough forms. Knead the dough for five to seven minutes, or until it is smooth and stretchy. The dough should be put in the fridge for at least 30 minutes after being wrapped in plastic wrap.
2. Make the filling for the shrimp: Cut the shrimp into small pieces and put them in a bowl with the ginger, soy sauce, sesame oil, black pepper, green onions, and cilantro. After mixing well, set it aside.
3. To put the wontons together, roll out the chilled dough into a thin sheet on a lightly floured surface. Cut circles out of the dough with a glass or a cookie cutter. Use a spoon to put some of the shrimp filling in the middle of each circle. I used water to brush the edges, then I folded the dough over to make a half-moon shape. Pinch the edges together to seal them.
4. To steam the wontons, put water in the basket of your electric steamer and heat it up until it starts to simmer. Place the wontons on the steamer rack so that there is space between them. Put the lid on top and steam for 12 to 15 minutes, or until the wontons are clear and fully cooked.
5. Set the dipping sauce aside while the wontons steam. In a small bowl, mix together all the ingredients for the dipping sauce. Mix everything together with a whisk, and then change the amount of spice to your liking.
6. Take a seat and enjoy: Place the steamed wontons on a platter to be served. As an extra touch, you can add chopped green onions and sesame seeds. Topping spicy shrimp wontons with sauce is a light and tasty way to eat them. Put the spicy sauce on the side and serve them.

34. STICKY TOFFEE PUDDING

Prep Time: 20 minutes | Cook Time: 45-50 minutes

Total Time: 65-70 minutes

Servings: 6-8

Ingredients

For the Pudding:

- 175g (¾ cup) packed light brown sugar
- 175g (6 ounce) pitted, chopped dates
- Pinch of salt
- 85g (3 ounce) softened butter
- 1 vanilla pod, split and seeds scraped
- 175ml (¾ cup boiling water
- 1 tbsp milk
- ½ tsp baking powder
- 175g (1¼ cup) self-raising flour
- 2 eggs

For the Caramel Sauce:

- 3 tbsp golden syrup
- 150ml (⅔ cup) double cream
- 100g (½ cup) packed light brown sugar
- 115g (½ cup) butter

Instructions

1. Put the chopped dates and boiling water in a saucepan. Turn down the heat and cook the vegetables for five minutes, or until they are soft. The vanilla pod and seeds should be included. Take it off the heat and let it cool down a bit.
2. Melt the fat and add the brown sugar. Warm the butter and add the brown sugar. Mix them together in a big bowl until they are light and fluffy.
3. Add the eggs one at a time, beating well after each one.
4. Putting in the dry stuff. In a different bowl, use a whisk to mix the flour, baking powder, and salt.
5. Get the batter together: Combine the cooled date mixture with the sugar and butter that has been creamed. Add the dry ingredients and milk one at a time, mixing just until combined. Don't mix too much.

6. To get ready to steam, grease individual ramekins or a dish that can go in the oven and can be used for steaming. Spread the batter out evenly in the ramekins. Add enough water to the steamer basket to come halfway up the sides of the ramekins.
7. Put the pudding in an electric steamer and heat it up. If you stick a skewer in the middle and it comes out clean, the pudding is done.
8. Mix the caramel sauce ingredients in a saucepan over medium-low heat while the pudding cooks. Bring it to a simmer and keep stirring it for 5 minutes, until it gets thick and bubbly. Take it off the heat and include the cream in a stir.
9. Assemble and enjoy: When the pudding is done steaming, take it out and let it cool for 5 minutes. You can either turn the ramekins upside down and serve the pudding from the dish. If necessary, slowly warm the caramel sauce in a saucepan and then pour it over the pudding. If you want, you can put vanilla ice cream or whipping cream on top of it. Have fun with your homemade warm caramel sauce and sticky toffee pudding!

35. STEAMED APPLE AND CRANBERRY CRUMBLE

Prep Time: 15 minutes | Cook Time: 30-35 minutes

Total Time: 45-50 minutes

Servings: 4-6

Ingredients

For the Apple and Cranberry Filling:

- 2 tbsp granulated sugar
- 1 tbsp cornstarch
- Pinch of grated nutmeg
- 4-5 medium apples, cored and sliced
- 1 cup of fresh cranberries
- 1/4 tsp ground cinnamon

For the Oat Crumble Topping:

- 1/4 cup of packed light brown sugar
- 1/4 cup of all-purpose flour
- Pinch of salt
- 1/4 cup of cold butter, cubed
- 1/2 cup of rolled oats

For Serving (Optional):

- Vanilla ice cream or whipped cream

Instructions

1. The filling needs to be made: Slowly add water to your electric steamer basket to heat it up. Spread the sliced apples, cranberries, sugar, cornstarch, cinnamon, and nutmeg out in a large bowl. Toss the apples and cranberries together. Roll in a way that covers everything.
2. Combine the oats, flour, brown sugar, cold cubed butter, and salt in a separate bowl to make the crumble topping. To make the dough look like loose crumbs, add the butter to the dry items and mix them together with your fingers or a pastry cutter.
3. Bring it all together and steam: If you have ramekins or a small ovenproof dish that can be used for steaming, divide the apple and cranberry mixture evenly between them. Over the fruit, sprinkle a lot of the crumble topping. Use the steamer basket to put the ramekins or dish in.
4. It takes 30 to 35 minutes of steaming, or until the apples are soft and the crumble topping is golden brown. Cover and steam the crumble.
5. Wait 5 to 10 minutes and then serve the crumble. Dollop vanilla ice cream or whipped cream on top of the bowls after scooping the mixture in. Eat your Steamed Apple and Cranberry Crumble, which is light and comforting.

36. SAVORY BEEF STEW WITH ROOT VEGETABLES

Prep Time: 20 minutes | Cook Time: 45 minutes

Total Time: 65 minutes

Servings: 4-6

Ingredients

For the Stew:

- 1 bay leaf
- 4 cups of beef broth
- 1 medium onion, chopped
- 1/2 tsp dried rosemary
- 1 tbsp tomato paste
- 2 carrots, peeled and chopped
- 1/4 tsp black pepper
- 2 parsnips, peeled and chopped
- 2 potatoes, peeled and chopped
- Salt to taste
- 1 pound beef stew meat, cut into bite-sized pieces
- 2 cloves garlic, minced
- 1 tsp dried thyme
- 1 tbsp olive oil
- 1 cup of red wine (optional)

For Serving (Optional):

- Crusty bread
- Chopped fresh parsley

Instructions

1. Put the olive oil in your pressure cooker and heat it over medium-high heat. Then brown the beef. Put in the beef chunks and cook them in groups, making sure all sides are well browned. Move the beef to a plate after it has browned.
2. Add the chopped onion, carrots, parsnips, and potatoes to the same pot and cook them until they are soft. Saute for 5 to 7 minutes, or until the vegetables get a little softer.
3. Put in the broth and spices: Add the salt, black pepper, thyme, and rosemary that has been chopped up. The red wine, tomato paste, bay leaf, and beef broth should all be added now. Bring to a low boil.
4. Cook under pressure: Put the browned beef back in the pot and cover it with the lid. For 45 minutes, cook on high pressure. Let the pressure drop naturally for 10 minutes, and then manually release any pressure that is still there.
5. Add salt and serve: Add salt to taste in the stew. You could add chopped fresh parsley on top if you'd like. Serve with crusty bread to dip. Root vegetable and beef stew is a hearty and tasty meal.

37. STEAMED CHICKEN AND VEGETABLE POTPOURRI

Prep Time: 20 minutes | Cook Time: 20-25 minutes

Total Time: 40-45 minutes

Servings: 4-6

Ingredients

For the Steamed Chicken and Vegetables:

- 1/4 tsp dried rosemary
- 1/4 tsp black pepper
- 1/2 cup of cherry tomatoes
- 1 pound boneless, skinless chicken breast, cut into bite-sized pieces
- 1/2 cup of chopped zucchini
- 1/2 cup of broccoli florets
- 1 onion, thinly sliced
- 1 bell pepper (red, yellow, or orange), sliced
- 1/4 cup of water
- 2 cloves garlic, minced
- 1/2 tsp dried thyme

For the Broth:

- 1 tsp olive oil
- 4 cups of chicken broth
- 1 tbsp lemon juice
- Salt to taste

For Serving (Optional):

- Cooked brown rice or quinoa
- Chopped fresh parsley or cilantro

Instructions

1. Get the broth ready. Put the chicken broth, lemon juice, olive oil, and salt in a bowl and whisk them together.
2. Get the vegetables ready: Cut the broccoli, zucchini, bell pepper, and cherry tomatoes into thin slices. Slice the onion and garlic very thin.
3. To make the potpourri, put the chicken pieces, sliced vegetables, onion, garlic, thyme, rosemary, and black pepper in a large bowl. Toss well to cover.
4. To steam the potpourri, fill your electric steamer basket with water and heat it until it starts to simmer. Put the chicken and vegetable mix in the steamer basket. Add the ready-made broth on top.
5. The chicken should be fully cooked and the vegetables should be soft but still crisp. Cover the steamer and steam for 20 to 25 minutes.
6. Take a seat and enjoy: Place the steamed potpourri on plates or a bowl for serving. As an extra touch, you can chop up fresh parsley or cilantro. For a full meal, serve with cooked brown rice or quinoa. Enjoy the journey's smells and tastes with each bite!

38. TROPICAL FRUIT AND COCONUT CREAM STEAMED

Prep Time: 20 minutes | Cook Time: 40-45 minutes

Total Time: 60-65 minutes

Servings: 4-6

Ingredients

For the Steamed Rice Pudding:

- 1 cup of white rice, rinsed
- 1/2 cup of water
- 1/4 cup of granulated sugar
- 1 1/2 cups of unsweetened coconut milk
- 1/4 tsp salt
- 1/2 tsp vanilla extract

For the Tropical Fruit Salad:

- 1/2 cup of fresh papaya, diced
- 1 cup of fresh mango, diced
- 1 tbsp lime juice
- 1 cup of fresh pineapple, diced
- 1/4 cup of kiwi, diced
- 1/4 cup of passion fruit pulp (optional)

For Serving (Optional):

- Whipped cream or toasted coconut flakes

Instructions

1. Mix the pudding ingredients together: Rinse the rice and put it in a large bowl. Add the coconut milk, water, sugar, salt, and vanilla extract.
2. Warm up the steamer: Put water in your electric steamer basket and then turn it down to a low heat.
3. Get the fruit salad ready: Dice the mango, pineapple, papaya, kiwi, and passion fruit pulp (if using) and put them all in a bowl. Add the lime juice and toss to keep from turning brown.
4. Warm the pudding up: Using a dish that has been lightly greased and can go in the oven, pour the rice mixture into it. Cover it with the fruit salad and spread it out evenly. Put the dish in the steamer basket with the lid on top.
5. Steam and decorate: Steam for 40 to 45 minutes, or until the pudding gets thick and the rice is cooked all the way through. Let it cool down a bit before you serve it.
6. Serve and enjoy: Put the steamed rice pudding into bowls. You can put whipped cream or toasted coconut flakes on top if you'd like. Enjoy the sweet and light island vacation with each scoop of fruity cream.

39. COMFORTING STEAMED CHICKEN NOODLE SOUP

Prep Time: 20 minutes | Cook Time: 25-30 minutes

Total Time: 45-50 minutes

Servings: 4-6

Ingredients

For the Broth:

- 1/2 tsp dried thyme
- 2 celery stalks, chopped
- 1 bay leaf
- 8 cups of chicken broth
- 1 pound boneless, skinless chicken breast, cut into bite-sized pieces
- 1/4 tsp dried parsley
- 2 carrots, peeled and chopped
- 1 onion, chopped
- 1 clove garlic, minced
- Salt and pepper to taste

For the Noodles:

- 12 ounces egg noodles

For Serving (Optional):

- Chopped fresh parsley or dill
- Lemon wedges
- Cooked brown rice or quinoa

Instructions

1. The chicken pieces, chicken broth, onion, carrots, celery, garlic, bay leaf, thyme, parsley, salt, and pepper should all be mixed together in a large bowl. Combine well to cover the chicken. To heat up the steamer, put water in the basket of your electric steamer and bring it to a simmer.
2. Steam the broth: Put the chicken and broth mixture in the steamer basket. The chicken should be cooked all the way through after 20 to 25 minutes of steaming.
3. In the meantime, cook the egg noodles the way the package says to. Once it's drained, set it aside.
4. Gather and serve: The bay leaf should be taken out of the broth. If you want a clear broth, you can throw away the chicken. If you want it to stay in the broth, shred it with two forks and add it back. Put in the cooked noodles and mix them in.
5. Add flowers and enjoy: Place bowls of the soothing steamed chicken noodle soup on the table. Add chopped fresh parsley or dill as a garnish if you want. For a full meal, serve with cooked brown rice or quinoa. Add more brightness by squeezing a lemon wedge into the bowl.

40. CINNAMON RAISIN STEAMED BUNS

Prep Time: 20 minutes | Cook Time: 15-20 minutes

Total Time: 1 hour 35 minutes

Servings: 12-15 buns

Ingredients

For the Dough:

- 3 tbsp granulated sugar
- 1/2 cup of warm milk (105°F-115°F)
- 3 cups of all-purpose flour
- 1 tbsp active dry yeast
- 1/4 tsp salt
- 1/4 cup of vegetable oil

For the Filling:

- 1/2 cup of packed light brown sugar
- 1/4 cup of raisins
- 2 tbsp ground cinnamon

For Brushing (Optional):

- 1 egg yolk beaten with 1 tbsp milk

Instructions

1. Mix the yeast with warm milk in a large bowl to get it going. Wait five minutes until it foams up. Make the dough. Mix the yeast with the sugar, salt, and 1 cup of flour. Mix everything together well. Knead the dough until it is smooth and easy to stretch. Adding the rest of the flour and oil slowly will make it better.
2. The dough needs to rise. Put it in a bowl that has been greased and cover it with plastic wrap. Leave it in a warm place for an hour, or until it has doubled in size.
3. Get the filling ready: Along with the raisins, put the brown sugar in a small bowl and mix them. Put the buns together: Flatten the dough with your hands and cut it into 12 to 15 equal pieces. Make a small ball out of each piece. Place your palm on top of each ball and press it down. Then, put a spoonful of jelly inside each one. To make a tight bun, pinch the edges together.
4. For the second rise, put the buns on a baking sheet or steamer basket that has been lightly greased. Leave space between them so they can rise. Put a lid on them and wait 30 minutes. To steam the buns, fill your electric steamer with water and heat it up until it starts to simmer. Put the baking sheet inside the steamer basket if you are using one. Put the lid on top and steam for 15 to 20 minutes, or until the buns are fluffy and fully cooked.
5. For a golden shine, brush the buns with the egg wash before steaming. You can also serve them right away. Fresh from the steamer, enjoy your warm and fluffy cinnamon raisin steamed buns!

SIDES DISHES

41. RAINBOW VEGGIE SPRING ROLLS

Prep Time: 20 minutes | Cook Time: 5 minutes

Total Time: 25 minutes

Servings: 6-8 spring rolls

Ingredients

For the Spring Rolls:

- 1/2 cup of fresh herbs
- 8 rice paper wrappers
- 1 cup of shredded yellow bell pepper
- 1 cup of shredded red bell pepper
- 1 cup of cucumber ribbons
- 1 cup of shredded carrots
- 1 cup of shredded red cabbage
- Handful of vermicelli noodles (optional)
- Cooked shrimp or tofu (optional)

For the Dipping Sauce:

- 2 tbsp lime juice
- 1 clove garlic, minced
- 1/4 cup of soy sauce
- 1 tsp honey
- 1 tbsp rice vinegar
- 1/2 tsp sriracha (optional)

Instructions

1. Get the vegetables ready: The carrots, bell peppers, cucumber, and cabbage should all be washed and then sliced or shred very thinly. Cut the fresh herbs up into little bits. If you're using vermicelli noodles, cook them according to the directions on the package. If you use shrimp or tofu, cook it first and then cut it up into small pieces.
2. How to make the dipping sauce: In a bowl, mix the soy sauce, rice vinegar, lime juice, honey, sriracha (if you want), and minced garlic with a whisk. Put away.
3. Put these things inside the spring rolls: Put a rice paper wrapper that has been slightly wet on a flat surface. In the middle of the wrapper, put a small handful of each vegetable, herb, and noodles (if you chose to use them). If you want, you can add cooked shrimp or tofu.
4. Serve and roll: Cover the filling with the bottom flap of the wrapper, and then fold the sides in tight. Carefully roll the wrapper up to cover the filling from top to bottom. Do it again with the rest of the wrappers and food.
5. If you want the filling to be a little softer and warmer, you can put the finished spring rolls in a steamer basket and steam them for three to five minutes.
6. Serve and have fun! Put the rainbow spring rolls on a plate and serve them with the sauce to dip them in. Enjoy the bright tastes and textures in every bite!

42. STEAMED ASPARAGUS WITH LEMON AND PARMESAN

Prep Time: 5 minutes | Cook Time: 3-5 minutes

Total Time: 8-10 minutes

Servings: 2-4

Ingredients

- 1/4 cup of freshly grated parmesan cheese
- 1/2 tbsp olive oil (optional)
- 1/4 tsp black pepper
- 1/2 lemon, juiced
- 1 pound asparagus, trimmed
- 1/4 tsp salt

Instructions

1. Get the asparagus ready by: Wash the asparagus and cut off any tough ends. You can peel the bottom third of the asparagus stalks to make them more tender if they are thick.
2. Bring the steamer up to temperature: Turn on your electric steamer and add water to the basket.
3. Optional: Season the asparagus with: Add the asparagus to a bowl and season it with salt, pepper, and olive oil (if you want).
4. Put the asparagus in boiling water: Make a single layer of asparagus in the steamer basket. Cover and steam for three to five minutes, depending on how thick the stalks are. If you stick a fork through them, they should be soft and crisp.
5. Serve on a plate: Move the steamed asparagus to a plate ready to serve. Add half a lemon's juice to the asparagus and then grated Parmesan cheese on top. Have fun right away!

43. CREAMY GARLIC MASHED POTATOES

Prep Time: 10 minutes | Cook Time: 20-25 minutes

Total Time: 30-35 minutes

Servings: 4-6

Ingredients

For the Mash:

- 2 pounds russet potatoes, peeled and cut into 1-inch cubes
- 1/2 cup of water
- 1/4 cup of unsalted butter, softened
- 2 cloves garlic, minced
- 1/2 tsp salt
- 1/4 tsp black pepper
- 1/4 cup of milk (optional)

For Serving (Optional):

- Chives, chopped parsley, or freshly cracked black pepper

Instructions

1. How to steam the potatoes: Put the cut potatoes and water in the basket of your electric steamer. It should be covered and steamed for 20 to 25 minutes, or until it is soft enough to pierce with a fork.
2. Put the garlic in a small saucepan and melt the butter over low heat while the potatoes are steaming. After you add the minced garlic, cook for about 30 seconds, until the garlic smells good but doesn't turn brown.
3. Mash the potatoes: Pat the steamed potatoes dry and squeeze out any extra water. Use a potato masher or a hand blender to smash them in a big bowl until they are smooth and creamy.
4. Taste and adjust: To the mashed potatoes, add the melted garlic butter, salt, and pepper. Thoroughly mix to combine. If you want a thinner consistency, add the milk slowly until you get the texture you want.
5. Assemble and enjoy: Put the garlic mashed potatoes that are creamy in a serving dish. You can top it with chopped chives, parsley, or freshly ground black pepper, but it's not necessary. Enjoy every bite of this light and flavorful comfort food!

44. HONEY SRIRACHA BRUSSELS SPROUTS

Prep Time: 10 minutes | Cook Time: 20-25 minutes

Total Time: 30-35 minutes

Servings: 4-6

Ingredients

- 1 pound Brussels sprouts, trimmed and halved
- 1 tbsp olive oil
- 1/2 tsp salt
- 1/4 tsp black pepper
- 2 tbsp honey
- 1 tbsp sriracha (adjust to your desired spice level)
- Optional toppings: Chopped fresh parsley, toasted sesame seeds, sriracha drizzle

Instructions

1. Put water in your electric steamer basket and then turn it down to a low heat.
2. Put the Brussels sprouts, salt, pepper, and olive oil in a bowl. Put them in the steamer basket and cover it. Steam for 10 to 15 minutes, or until crisp and tender.
3. Move the Brussels sprouts to a serving dish once they are soft but still crisp. Add the honey-sriracha glaze and gently toss to coat.
4. Add chopped fresh parsley, toasted sesame seeds, or an extra drizzle of Sriracha (if you want) and enjoy!

45. STEAMED QUINOA WITH HERBS AND NUTS

Prep Time: 10 minutes | Cook Time: 15-20 minutes

Total Time: 25-30 minutes

Servings: 4-6

Ingredients

- 1 1/2 cups of water or broth (vegetable, chicken, etc.)
- 1/4 cup of chopped nuts (almonds, walnuts, pecans, pistachios, or a combination)
- 1 cup of quinoa, rinsed
- 1/4 tsp salt
- 1/4 tsp black pepper
- 1/4 cup of chopped fresh herbs (parsley, cilantro, mint, basil, or a combination)
- Optional toppings: Chopped fresh chives, crumbled feta cheese, avocado slices, dried cranberries, a drizzle of olive oil or lemon juice

Instructions

1. Add the quinoa and liquid together. Put the rinsed quinoa, water or broth, salt, and pepper in a bowl. Mix well by stirring.
2. To steam the quinoa, put the quinoa mixture in the basket of your electric steamer. Put the lid on top and steam for 15 to 20 minutes, or until the quinoa is fluffy and cooked all the way through. It should soak up the liquid.
3. When the quinoa is done, take it out of the steamer basket and use a fork to fluff it up. Let it cool down. Allow it to cool a bit.
4. Try and make changes: If you think the quinoa needs more salt and pepper, give it a try.
5. Add nuts and herbs: Add the chopped fresh herbs and nuts. Mix slowly to combine, but don't mix too much.
6. Take a seat and enjoy: Put the quinoa that has been steamed with nuts and herbs on a serving dish. Add any toppings you like (optional), and enjoy the light and tasty dish!

46. SAVORY SUN-KISSED BROCCOLINI

Prep Time: 10 minutes | Cook Time: 15-20 minutes

Total Time: 25-30 minutes

Servings: 4-6

Ingredients

For the Broccolini:

- 1/2 tsp salt
- 1 pound fresh broccolini, trimmed and cut into 2-inch pieces
- 1/4 tsp black pepper
- 1 tbsp olive oil
- 1/4 tsp crushed red pepper flakes (optional)

For the Beans:

- 2 cloves garlic, minced
- 1/4 cup of vegetable broth
- 1/4 cup of chopped fresh parsley
- 1/4 cup of freshly grated Parmesan cheese
- 1 (15 ounce) can cannellini beans, drained and rinsed
- Pinch of red pepper flakes (optional)

Instructions

1. To steam the broccolini, put it in the basket of your electric steamer. Add olive oil and salt, pepper, and red pepper flakes (if you want) to taste. For 5 to 7 minutes, or until crisp-tender, cover and steam.
2. Get the beans ready: Set a pan on medium heat while you wait. After you add the garlic, cook for 30 seconds or until it smells good. You can add red pepper flakes, parsley, vegetable broth, and white beans if you want to. Turn the heat down to low and cook for two to three minutes, until everything is warm.
3. Put together and serve: Move the broccolini from the steamer to a serving dish. Place the garlicky white beans on top and sprinkle Parmesan cheese on top of them. Warm it up and enjoy the sun-kissed flavors!

47. GARLICKY SICHUAN EDAMAME WITH TOASTED SESAME

Prep Time: 5 minutes | Cook Time: 5 minutes

Total Time: 10 minutes

Servings: 2-3

Ingredients

- 2 tbsp toasted sesame seeds
- Pinch of Sichuan peppercorns (optional)
- 1/2 tsp rice vinegar
- 1/4 tsp red pepper flakes (adjust to your spice preference)
- 1 cup of frozen edamame, thawed
- 1/4 tsp minced garlic
- 1 tbsp toasted sesame oil
- 1/8 tsp ground ginger
- 1 tsp soy sauce

Instructions

1. Make the edamame steam by adding water to the steamer basket and letting it heat up slowly. Put the thawed edamame in the basket and put the lid on top. Do this for three to five minutes, or until everything is hot.
2. Get the sauce ready: In a small bowl, mix the sesame oil, soy sauce, rice vinegar, garlic, ginger, Sichuan peppercorns (if using), and red pepper flakes with a whisk while the edamame steams.
3. Throw and serve: Move the edamame from the steamer to a bowl for serving. Add the ready-made sauce and toss to coat. Add some toasted sesame seeds on top. Enjoy the sour Sichuan flavors!

48. STEAMED CORN ON THE COB WITH GARLIC HERB

Prep Time: 5 minutes | Cook Time: 8-10 minutes

Total Time: 13-15 minutes

Servings: 4-6

Ingredients

For the Corn:

- 4 ears fresh corn, husks removed and silks cleaned
- Water (for steaming)

For the Garlic Herb Butter:

- 1/2 cup of softened butter
- 2 cloves garlic, minced
- 1/4 cup of chopped fresh herbs (parsley, cilantro, basil, chives, or a combination)
- 1/2 tsp salt
- 1/4 tsp black pepper
- Pinch of red pepper flakes (optional)

Instructions

1. Get the steamer ready: Put water in your electric steamer basket and then turn it down to a low heat.
2. To steam the corn, put the cobs in the steamer basket and try to keep them standing up. If you cover it, steam it for 8 to 10 minutes, or until it's crisp and soft.
3. To make the herb and garlic butter: In a bowl, cream the softened butter, minced garlic, chopped herbs, salt, pepper, and (if you want) red pepper flakes together until smooth and tasty. Do this while the corn is steaming.
4. Take a seat and enjoy: Place the steamed corn cobs on a platter to serve. Spread a lot of the garlicky herb butter on each cob and let it melt a bit on top of the hot corn. Indulge in the juicy, tasty corn and enjoy every bite!

49. MEDITERRANEAN BLISS WITH CAPERS AND FETA

Prep Time: 10 minutes | Cook Time: 20-25 minutes

Total Time: 30-35 minutes

Servings: 4-6

Ingredients

For Roasting:

- 1/2 tsp salt
- 1 tbsp olive oil
- 2 red bell peppers
- 1/4 tsp black pepper
- 2 large tomatoes

For the Salad:

- 2 tbsp red wine vinegar
- 1/2 cup of crumbled feta cheese
- 1/4 cup of chopped Kalamata olives
- 2 tbsp capers, drained
- 1/4 cup of fresh parsley, chopped
- 1 tbsp olive oil
- 1/4 cup of chopped red onion

Instructions

1. To heat up your steamer, put water in the basket and bring it to a simmer.
2. Get the vegetables ready by: Warm your oven up to 200°C (400°F). Cut the tomatoes and peppers in half and throw away the seeds and stems. Sprinkle salt and pepper on them and add olive oil on top. Then, put them in the steamer basket cut side down. To make the vegetables soft and a little smoky, cover them and steam them for 15 to 20 minutes.
3. You can choose to roast the vegetables: You can move the vegetables to a baking sheet and roast them in a hot oven for 5 to 10 minutes to give them a little more char and caramelization while they steam.
4. Put together the salad: Crumble the feta cheese and chop the red onion, olives, and parsley while the vegetables cool a bit.
5. In a tiny bowl, combine the olive oil and red wine vinegar together with a whisk.
6. Toss and serve: Put the roasted tomatoes and peppers on a platter to serve. Add the red onion, olives, feta cheese, and parsley on top of them. Spread the dressing over the salad and gently toss to mix. Enjoy the sour and bright flavors of the Mediterranean!

50. CLASSIC GARLICKY BEANS WITH TOASTED ALMONDS

Prep Time: 5 minutes | Cook Time: 10-15 minutes

Total Time: 15-20 minutes

Servings: 4-6

Ingredients

- 1 tbsp olive oil
- 2 cloves garlic, minced
- 1 pound fresh green beans, trimmed and halved
- 1/2 cup of slivered almonds
- 1/4 tsp salt
- 1/4 tsp black pepper
- Optional toppings: Chopped fresh parsley, lemon zest, crumbled feta cheese

Instructions

1. Turn on your electric steamer and add water to the basket.
2. Combine the green beans, garlic, and olive oil in a bowl.
3. Cover and put the green beans in the steamer basket. For 8 to 10 minutes, or until tender but crisp, steam.
4. Almonds must be toasted in a dry pan over medium-low heat until they turn golden brown and smell good while the beans are cooking.
5. To serve, put the steamed green beans, toasted almonds, salt, and pepper in a bowl. Roll in to coat. Add the toppings you want (optional), and enjoy!

51. HONEY BALSAMIC GLAZED SWEET POTATOES

Prep Time: 10 minutes | Cook Time: 15-20 minutes

Total Time: 25-30 minutes

Servings: 4-6

Ingredients

- 2 tbsp honey
- 1 tbsp olive oil
- 2 large sweet potatoes, peeled and cut into 1-inch cubes
- 1/4 tsp salt
- 1/4 tsp black pepper
- 1/4 cup of balsamic vinegar
- 1/4 cup of chopped pecans, toasted

Instructions

1. Put water in your electric steamer basket and then turn it down to low heat.
2. In a bowl, stir the sweet potato cubes with salt, pepper, and olive oil.
3. Cover the steamer basket and add the sweet potatoes that have been coated. Steam them for 15 to 20 minutes or until they're soft and a fork works through them without any trouble.
4. In a small saucepan, mix the honey and balsamic vinegar with a whisk while the sweet potatoes steam. Bring to a simmer over medium-low heat. Cook for 5-7 minutes or until it gets a little thicker and less liquid.
5. The steamed sweet potatoes and pecans should be mixed together in a serving bowl. Pour the balsamic glaze over the food and gently toss to coat.
6. Enjoy the sweet and sour taste with the satisfying crunch of the toasted pecans.

52. PROVENÇAL SUNSHINE WITH FRESH HERBS

Prep Time: 15 minutes | Cook Time: 20-25 minutes

Total Time: 35-40 minutes

Servings: 4-6

Ingredients

For the Vegetables:

- 1/2 tsp salt
- 1/4 tsp dried thyme
- 1 yellow bell pepper, cubed
- 1 medium yellow squash, cubed
- 1 medium eggplant, cubed
- 1 red bell pepper, cubed
- 1 tbsp olive oil
- 1 medium zucchini, cubed
- 1/4 tsp black pepper
- 1/4 tsp dried oregano
- 1 large tomato, peeled and chopped

For the Finishing Touches:

- 1/4 cup of chopped fresh parsley
- 1/4 cup of chopped fresh basil
- 1/4 cup of toasted pine nuts
- Extra virgin olive oil (for drizzling)

Instructions

1. Put water in your electric steamer basket and then turn it down to low heat.
2. Put the tomato, bell peppers, zucchini, eggplant, and zucchini cubes in a bowl. Add the olive oil, salt, pepper, thyme, and oregano.
3. Cover the steamer basket and add the vegetables that have been coated. Steam them for 15 to 20 minutes or until they are soft and crisp but still have their shape.
4. Set the pine nuts in a dry pan over medium-low flame and toast them until they turn golden brown and smell good.
5. Put the steamed vegetables, parsley, basil, and toasted pine nuts in a serving bowl. Place a little extra virgin olive oil and toss the salad gently to mix.
6. Enjoy the bright flavors of Provence and the great contrast in texture between the soft vegetables and the crunchy pine nuts.

53. PROVENÇAL SUN-KISSED SPINACH

Prep Time: 5 minutes | Cook Time: 10-12 minutes

Total Time: 15-17 minutes

Servings: 4-6

Ingredients

- 1 tbsp olive oil
- 1/4 tsp black pepper
- 1/2 tsp salt
- 2 cloves garlic, minced
- 1/4 cup of freshly squeezed lemon juice
- 1 pound fresh baby spinach, washed and dried
- 1/4 cup of toasted pine nuts

Instructions

1. To steam the spinach, put water in your electric steamer basket and heat it until it just starts to simmer. Cover the spinach in the basket. For three to five minutes, or until soft and wilted, steam.
2. Get the dressing ready: Put the olive oil in a small pan and heat it over medium-low heat while the spinach steams. Put in the garlic and bake for 30 seconds, until it smells good. Turn the heat up to low and add the lemon juice, salt, and pepper. Stir it all in.
3. Put together and serve: Move the spinach from the steamer to a bowl for serving. Toss the spinach to coat it with the warm dressing. For a sun-kissed taste, sprinkle with toasted pine nuts.

54. STEAMED CAULIFLOWER RICE WITH PARMESAN

Prep Time: 5 minutes | Cook Time: 10-12 minutes

Total Time: 15-17 minutes

Servings: 4-6

Ingredients

- 1 head cauliflower, trimmed and florets cut into small pieces
- 1/2 cup of vegetable broth (or chicken broth for richer flavor)
- 2 tbsp chopped fresh parsley (or other herbs like basil, chives, dill)
- 1/4 cup of grated Parmesan cheese
- 1 clove garlic, minced
- 1 tbsp olive oil
- Salt and pepper to taste

Instructions

1. In the electric steamer basket, put the cauliflower florets. Put water in the base and heat it up for 8 to 10 minutes or until soft but still crunchy; steam the cauliflower.
2. Put the olive oil in a large skillet and heat it over medium-low heat while the cauliflower steams. Put in the garlic and bake for 30 seconds, until it smells good.
3. Move the cauliflower to the pan with the garlic after it's done cooking. Put in the vegetable broth and raise the heat. Cook for two to three minutes or until the broth is almost gone.
4. Take the pan off the heat and add the parsley, salt, and pepper, and then stir them in. Mix everything together, and serve right away.

55. HONEY GLAZED CARROTS WITH PECANS

Prep Time: 5 minutes | Cook Time: 10 minutes

Total Time: 15 minutes

Servings: 4-6

Ingredients

- 1/4 cup of unsalted butter, melted
- Pinch of salt
- 1 pound carrots, peeled and trimmed
- 1/4 tsp ground cinnamon
- 1/4 cup of honey
- 1/4 cup of chopped pecans

Instructions

1. Put water in the bottom of your electric steamer and heat it up. Put the carrots in the steamer basket and steam them for 8 to 10 minutes or until they are soft but still crisp.
2. Melt the butter and put the honey, cinnamon, and salt in a small bowl. Whisk the ingredients together while the carrots are steaming.
3. After the carrots are cooked, take them out of the steamer and put them on a dish to serve. Add the honey glaze to the carrots and gently toss to coat.
4. Add the chopped pecans to the carrots that have been glazed, and serve right away.

56. STEAMED BROCCOLI WITH SESAME GINGER

Prep Time: 5 minutes | Cook Time: 10-12 minutes

Total Time: 15-17 minutes

Servings: 4-6

Ingredients

For the Broccoli:

- 1 head broccoli, trimmed and florets cut into bite-sized pieces
- 1/4 cup of water (optional)

For the Sesame Ginger Dressing:

- 1 tbsp honey or maple syrup
- 2 tbsp rice vinegar or apple cider vinegar
- 1/2 tsp sriracha (optional, for spice)
- 1 tbsp toasted sesame seeds
- 1 tsp grated ginger
- 1 tbsp soy sauce (reduced-sodium preferred)
- 1 tbsp toasted sesame oil
- 1 clove garlic, minced

Instructions

Steam the Broccoli:

1. Put water on the bottom of your electric steamer. If you want the broccoli flavor to be stronger, you can steam it without water. Bring up the temperature.
2. Cover the broccoli and put the florets in the steamer basket.
3. Depending on your taste, steam for 5 to 7 minutes or until tender-crisp.

Make the Sesame Ginger Dressing:

1. Gather the dressing ingredients in a small bowl and mix them well with a whisk while the broccoli cooks.

Assemble and Serve:

1. Move the broccoli from the steamer to a serving dish.
2. Pour the sesame ginger dressing over the broccoli and gently toss it to cover it.
3. Add more toasted sesame seeds as a garnish if you want to.
4. Serve right away while still warm.
5.

57. ROASTED PUMPKIN AND FETA SALAD

Prep Time: 10 minutes | Cook Time: 15 minutes

Total Time: 25 minutes

Servings: 4-6

Ingredients

For the Pumpkin:

- 1 small pie pumpkin (or butternut squash), halved and seeds removed
- Salt and pepper to taste
- 1 tbsp olive oil

For the Salad:

- 1/2 cup of crumbled feta cheese
- 4 cups of mixed greens (arugula, spinach, kale, etc.)
- 1/4 cup of pumpkin seeds
- 1/2 red onion, thinly sliced
- 1/4 cup of dried cranberries (optional)

For the Balsamic Vinaigrette:

- 1/2 tsp honey
- Salt and pepper to taste
- 1 tsp Dijon mustard
- 2 tbsp balsamic vinegar
- 1 tbsp olive oil

Instructions

Steam the Pumpkin:

1. Put water in the bottom of your electric steamer and heat it up.
2. Add salt and pepper to the pumpkin halves and brush them with olive oil.
3. Put the pumpkin halves in the steamer basket so that the flesh side is facing down.
4. It should be steamed for 12 to 15 minutes or until it is soft and tender.

Prepare the Salad:

1. Mix the greens, red onion, and pumpkin seeds in a large bowl while the pumpkin steams.

Make the Balsamic Vinaigrette:

1. Olive oil, honey, and balsamic vinegar should all be mixed together in a small bowl using a whisk. Add pepper and salt to taste.

Assemble and Serve:

1. Take the pumpkin out of the steamer and let it cool down a bit after it's done cooking. The meat should be broken up into small pieces and put in the salad bowl.
2. Put the crumbled feta cheese on the salad and, if you want, sprinkle with dried cranberries. Add the balsamic vinaigrette to the salad and gently toss to mix. Serving right away.

58. STEAMED ZUCCHINI AND YELLOW SQUASH

Prep Time: 5 minutes | Cook Time: 10-12 minutes

Total Time: 15-17 minutes

Servings: 4-6

Ingredients

- 1 tbsp olive oil
- 1/4 cup of chopped fresh herbs (basil, parsley, dill, mint, chives, or a combination)
- 1 medium yellow squash, sliced thinly
- 1 medium zucchini, sliced thinly
- Salt and pepper to taste
- 1 clove garlic, minced (optional)
- Lemon zest (optional)

Instructions

Prepare the Zucchini and Squash:

1. Carefully clean and cut the yellow and zucchini squash. For even cooking, cut them into fourths that are about 1/4 inch thick and on the diagonal.

Steam the Vegetables:

1. Put water in the bottom of your electric steamer and heat it up.
2. In the steamer basket, put the slices of zucchini and yellow squash.
3. Depending on your taste, steam for 5 to 7 minutes or until tender-crisp.

Combine and Season:

1. Move the vegetables from the steamer to a bowl for serving.
2. Sprinkle with olive oil and, if using, garlic. Toss gently to add the coating.
3. For extra flavor, add chopped herbs, salt, and pepper.
4. Optional: squeeze in some lemon zest to make it even brighter.

Serve:

1. For best results, serve the steamed squash and zucchini warm or at room temperature. This is good as a side dish or a light starter.

59. STEAMED ARTICHOKES WITH LEMON BUTTER DIP

Prep Time: 10 minutes | Cook Time: 20-40 minutes

Total Time: 30-50 minutes

Servings: 4-6

Ingredients

For the Artichokes:

- Water
- 4 large globe artichokes
- Lemon juice (from 1-2 lemons)

For the Lemon Butter Dip:

- 1/2 tsp garlic powder
- 2 tbsp lemon juice
- Salt and pepper to taste
- 1/4 cup of chopped fresh parsley (or other herbs like dill, chives, tarragon)
- 1/2 cup of (1 stick) unsalted butter, softened

Instructions

Prepare the Artichokes:

1. Put about 2 inches of water in a big pot and squeeze the juice of one lemon into it.
2. Cut off the artichokes' stems and about an inch of the tough leaves on the outside. Cut off the pointy ends of the rest of the leaves with kitchen scissors.
3. To keep the cut pieces from turning brown, rub them with lemon juice.
4. Place the artichokes in the pot so that the stem ends are facing up. Use a steamer basket or trivet to keep them stable if they don't stand up straight on their own.

Steam the Artichokes:

1. When the water starts to boil, turn down the heat and cover the pot.
2. The artichokes should be steamed for 20 to 40 minutes or until the stem can be cut and the leaves are easy to pull off. How long they take to cook will depend on how big they are.

Prepare the Lemon Butter Dip:

1. It's time to make the sauce. In a small dish, mix the softened butter, chopped parsley, lemon juice, garlic powder, salt, and pepper. Beat the mixture until it's smooth and creamy.

Serve:

1. Prior to serving, let the artichokes cool down a bit.
2. Carefully peel off each leaf, then dip the base in the lemon butter sauce and use your teeth to scrape off the flesh.
3. Getting to the heart of the artichoke, throw away the fuzzy choke in the middle. Savor the soft heart while dipping it in the tasty sauce.

60. GRILLED FRUIT SKEWERS WITH HONEY YOGURT

Prep Time: 10 minutes | Cook Time: 10-15 minutes

Total Time: 20-25 minutes

Servings: 4-6

Ingredients

For the Fruit Skewers:

- 1 pineapple, cored and cut into chunks
- 1 mango, peeled and cut into chunks
- 2 plums, pitted and cut into wedges
- 1/2 tsp ground cinnamon
- Wooden skewers
- 1/4 tsp ground ginger (optional)
- 2 peaches, pitted and cut into wedges
- 1/4 cup of brown sugar

For the Honey Yogurt Drizzle:

- 1 tbsp lemon juice
- 2 tbsp honey
- Pinch of ground cardamom (optional)
- 1 cup of plain Greek yogurt

Instructions

1. All fruits should be washed and dried. Cut them into pieces of about the same size that can be threaded onto skewers.
2. Put brown sugar, cinnamon, and ginger (if using) in a small bowl and mix them together. Toss the fruit pieces in the spice mix so that they are all covered.
3. Put water in the bottom of your electric steamer and heat it up.
4. Using different colors and textures of fruit to make the skewers look more interesting, thread the pieces of fruit onto them. Close the lid and put the fruit skewers in the steamer basket.
5. Steam the fruits for 5 to 7 minutes or until they get warm and a little soft. The skewers can also be lightly grilled on a hot grill pan to add a little smoke flavor before they are steamed.
6. In a small bowl, stir the yogurt, honey, lemon juice, and cardamom (if using) with a whisk until smooth and creamy. Turn the fruit on high heat.
7. Put the fruit skewers that have been steamed on plates. Spread the honey yogurt sauce all over the food. For a cool dessert, serve right away while still warm or chilled.

MAIN COURSES

61. SPICY KOREAN BEEF BULGOGI BOWL

Prep Time: 15 minutes | Cook Time: 15 minutes

Total Time: 30 minutes

Servings: 4

Ingredients

For the Spicy Korean Beef Bulgogi:

- 1 tbsp gochujang
- 1 tbsp garlic, minced
- 1/2 tsp black pepper
- 1 tbsp ginger, minced
- 1/2 pound lean beef flank steak, thinly sliced against the grain
- 1 tbsp sesame oil
- 1 tbsp brown sugar
- 2 tbsp soy sauce
- 1/4 tsp Korean BBQ spice (optional)

For the Bulgogi Bowl:

- 2 cups of cooked white rice
- 1 scallion, thinly sliced
- 1/2 cucumber, thinly sliced
- 1 tbsp toasted sesame seeds
- 1 cup of kimchi, chopped

For the Sesame Scallion Sauce:

- 2 tbsp soy sauce
- 1/4 tsp garlic powder
- 1/2 tsp sriracha (optional)
- 1 tbsp rice vinegar
- Pinch of black pepper
- 1 tbsp sesame oil
- 1 tsp honey

Instructions

1. Put all of the ingredients for the Spicy Korean Beef Bulgogi into a large bowl and mix them together. Add the sliced beef and mix it in well to cover it all. Cover and let it sit for at least 15 minutes. If you want a stronger flavor, let it sit for up to 30 minutes.
2. Put water in the bottom of your electric steamer and heat it up. Put the beef that has been marinated in the steamer basket for 8-10 minutes, or until cooked all the way through and just a little soft, steam.
3. As the beef steams, follow the directions on the package to cook the white rice. Put the cooked rice into bowls. Kimchi, cucumber slices, and steamed beef should be put on top.
4. Mix the Sesame Scallion Sauce ingredients in a small bowl with a whisk. Pour the sauce over the bowls. Add toasted sesame seeds and sliced scallions to the top of each bowl. Serve right away while still hot.

62. HONEY GARLIC SALMON WITH BROCCOLI

Prep Time: 10 minutes | Cook Time: 15 minutes

Total Time: 25 minutes

Servings: 4

Ingredients

For the Salmon:

- 1 tsp garlic, minced
- 1/2 tsp ginger, minced
- 1 tbsp rice vinegar
- 1/4 cup of soy sauce
- 2 tbsp honey
- 4 salmon fillets (4-6 ounce each), skin on or off
- 1/4 tsp black pepper
- 2 tbsp brown sugar

For the Broccoli:

- 1 head broccoli, cut into florets

Instructions

1. Mix the brown sugar, garlic, ginger, soy sauce, honey, and black pepper in a small bowl with a whisk. Put away.
2. Put the salmon fillets in a dish that is not too deep. Make sure to cover both sides of the salmon with half of the honey garlic glaze. While you make the broccoli, let the meat sit for 10 minutes.
3. Put water in the bottom of your electric steamer and heat it up. Cover the broccoli and put the florets in the steamer basket. Steam for 5 to 7 minutes or until crisp and tender.
4. Take the broccoli out of the steamer basket and set it aside. Place the salmon fillets in the basket so that the skin side is facing down. Spread the salmon with the rest of the honey garlic glaze. If you use a fork to flake the salmon, it means it's fully cooked. Steam for 7 to 9 minutes.
5. Place the broccoli that has been steamed on each plate. Place the cooked salmon on top, and then pour any glaze that's left over from the bottom of the dish over the fish and broccoli.

63. STEAMED CHICKEN AND DUMPLINGS

Prep Time: 15 minutes | Cook Time: 25-30 minutes

Total Time: 40-45 minutes

Servings: 4-6

Ingredients

For the Broth:

- 6 cups of chicken broth (or vegetable broth for vegetarian option)
- 2 celery stalks, thinly sliced
- Salt and pepper to taste
- 4 sprigs fresh thyme
- 2 bay leaves
- 2 carrots, peeled and thinly sliced
- 1 onion, peeled and quartered

For the Chicken:

- 1 pound boneless, skinless chicken breasts or thighs, cut into bite-sized pieces

For the Dumplings:

- 1/4 tsp salt
- 1/4 cup of chopped fresh parsley (or other herbs like dill, chives, tarragon)
- 1/4 cup of cold butter, cubed
- 1/2 cup of buttermilk or milk
- 1 1/2 cups of all-purpose flour
- 1/2 tsp baking powder

Instructions

1. Put the onion, carrots, celery, salt, pepper, thyme sprigs, bay leaves, and chicken broth in a large pot. Once it starts to simmer, lower the flame and let it cook for 10 minutes. This will let the flavors soak in.
2. Put the chicken pieces into the broth that is already simmering. Cook for 10 to 15 minutes or until the chicken is fully cooked. The chicken should be taken out of the pot and set aside.
3. Within a dish about the size of a dinner plate, mix salt, flour, and baking powder. Combine everything with a whisk. Prepare the bowl by chopping the parsley into small pieces. To make the dough look like big crumbs, put the cold butter and mix it with the dry ingredients. Forks or a pastry cutter are both good options.
4. Incorporate the milk or buttermilk slowly while mixing until a soft dough forms. Assemble the ingredients well.
5. Flatten the dough out on a surface that has been lightly dusted with flour until it is about 1/4 inch thick. Cut it into squares with a knife or use a biscuit cutter to make rounds. For more moisture, add a little broth to the bottom of each dumpling.
6. Heat the steamer basket over the simmering broth. As you put the dumplings in the steamer basket, make sure there is space between them. Dumplings should be fluffy and cooked all the way through after 8 to 10 minutes of steaming.
7. The cooked chicken should be put back in the pot with the dumplings and broth. Stir slowly, and if you need to, change the seasonings. Serve the warm and comforting chicken and dumplings with herb broth in bowls.

64. STEAMED DIM SUM

Prep Time: 30-60 minutes | Cook Time: 10-15 minutes

Total Time: 40-75 minutes

Servings: 4-6

Ingredients

Dumplings:

- Siu Mai (pork and shrimp dumplings)
- Vegetable Dumplings (with variety of fillings like bok choy, mushrooms, carrots)
- Har Gow (shrimp dumplings)
- Ha Cheung (steamed rice rolls)

Buns:

- Da Bao (vegetable buns)
- Char Siu Bao (steamed barbecue pork buns)
- Xia Long Bao (soup dumplings)

Pastries:

- Har Gow Cheung (steamed rice flour rolls)
- Wu Gok (pan-fried turnip cake)
- Cheung Fen (rice noodle rolls)

Instructions

1. Follow the directions on the package or in the recipe for the dim sum you want to make. To keep from leaking while steaming, make sure that all the pieces are properly sealed.
2. Warm up your electric steamer. Add enough water or chicken broth to the base of the steamer to make a thin layer of steaming liquid.
3. Put the dim sum that you've already made in the steamer basket(s). Keep an eye on the spacing to make sure the steaming is even. Depending on how much dim sum you have, you may need to use more than one tier.
4. Place the lid on top of the steamer and steam for 10 to 15 minutes, or until the dim sum is fully cooked and has a slight sheen to it. The time it takes to cook may change based on the size and filling of the dim sum you choose.
5. Serve your tasty Electric Steamer Steamed Dim Sum right away while it's still hot. Enjoy with your favorite dipping sauces and enjoy the wide range of tastes and textures!

65. LEMON GARLIC CHICKEN AND ASPARAGUS

Prep Time: 10 minutes | Cook Time: 12-15 minutes

Total Time: 22-25 minutes

Servings: 4

Ingredients

For the Chicken:

- 2 tbsp soy sauce
- 2 tbsp lemon juice
- 1/4 cup of olive oil
- 1 tsp garlic powder
- Salt and pepper to taste
- 4 boneless, skinless chicken breasts or thighs (thinly sliced or pounded)
- 1 tbsp Worcestershire sauce
- 1/2 tsp dried oregano

For the Asparagus:

- 1 pound asparagus, trimmed and cut into 1-inch pieces

Optional Garnishes:

- Sliced almonds
- Lemon wedges
- Chopped fresh parsley

Instructions

1. The soy sauce, Worcestershire sauce, garlic powder, oregano, salt, and pepper should all be mixed together in a large bowl using a whisk. Put the chicken pieces and toss them around to make sure they are evenly covered. Leave it to sit for at least 10 minutes or up to 30 minutes if you want it to taste even better.
2. Get water to a boil and put it in the bottom of your electric steamer.
3. Put the chicken pieces that have been marinated in the steamer basket so that they don't touch each other. Place the lid on top and steam for 8 to 10 minutes, or until the food is fully cooked and the juices barely run.
4. Put the asparagus in a separate bowl while the chicken is steaming. Insert a plate on top of the bowl and add a little water or broth for one to two minutes on high or until tender-crisp. You could also put the asparagus in the steamer basket with the chicken for the last two to three minutes of cooking.
5. Plate up the cooked chicken and asparagus. Take out any extra marinade from

66. MEDITERRANEAN BLISS WITH LEMON, TOMATOES

Prep Time: 10 minutes | Cook Time: 15-20 minutes

Total Time: 25-30 minutes

Servings: 2-3

Ingredients

For the Fish:

- Salt and pepper to taste
- 1 tbsp olive oil
- 2 fish fillets (cod, salmon, or snapper work well)

For the Parchment Packets:

- 1 tomato, thinly sliced
- 2 large sheets of parchment paper
- 1/4 cup of Kalamata olives, pitted and sliced
- 2 cloves garlic, minced
- 1 red bell pepper, thinly sliced
- 1 lemon, sliced
- 1/4 cup of chopped fresh basil
- 1/4 cup of chopped fresh parsley
- 1/4 cup of white wine (optional)

Instructions

1. Fill the basket with water and bring it to a simmer to heat up your steamer.
2. On top of the fish fillets, sprinkle them with olive oil and salt and pepper.
3. Put half of the tomato slices, olives, garlic, parsley, basil, lemon slices, and bell pepper slices on each piece of parchment paper. On top of each bed of herbs and vegetables, put a fish fillet.
4. Put two tbsp of white wine into each packet if you want to use it. To seal the packets, fold the parchment paper into triangles and crimp the edges together tightly.
5. Cover the steamer basket and put the parchment parcels inside. Put the fish in the steamer for 15 to 20 minutes or until it's fully cooked and flaky when you use a fork.
6. Open the bags carefully, then move the vegetables and fish to plates. Add any pan juices on top, and enjoy the bright Mediterranean flavors!

67. SPICY BLACK BEAN BURGERS

Prep Time: 15 minutes | Cook Time: 15-20 minutes

Total Time: 30-35 minutes

Servings: 4-6 patties

Ingredients

- 1 clove garlic, minced
- 1/2 cup of cooked brown rice or quinoa
- 1/4 cup of chopped sweet pepper (Jalapeno for extra spice)
- 1/4 tsp chili powder
- 1/4 tsp smoked paprika
- 1/4 cup of chopped fresh cilantro
- 1 (15 ounce) can black beans, drained and rinsed
- 1/4 cup of diced red onion
- 1/2 tsp ground cumin
- Pinch of cayenne pepper (optional)
- Salt and pepper to taste
- 1/4 cup of panko breadcrumbs (optional)

Instructions

1. Set your steamer basket on high heat and add just enough water to cover it.
2. Use a food processor to chop the black beans, rice or quinoa, onion, pepper, garlic, cilantro, and spices into small pieces. Stay within a reasonable distance; you want some texture!
3. Add pepper and salt to the mixture after moving it to a bowl. If you need to, add breadcrumbs to make it easier to form patties.
4. Make patty-shaped balls out of 4 to 6 equal parts of the mixture.
5. Cover the steamer basket and put the patties in it. Steam for 15 to 20 minutes or until hot all the way through and a little firm.

68. CLASSIC TERIYAKI WITH SESAME AND TOASTED ALMONDS

Prep Time: 10 minutes | Cook Time: 15-20 minutes

Total Time: 25-30 minutes

Servings: 4-6

Ingredients

For the Chicken:

- 1/2 tsp salt
- 1 pound boneless, skinless chicken breasts, sliced into thin strips
- 1/4 tsp black pepper
- 1 tbsp cornstarch

For the Teriyaki Glaze:

- 1/4 cup of soy sauce
- 1 tbsp rice vinegar
- 1 clove garlic, minced
- 1 tsp honey
- 1/2 tsp ginger, minced
- 1/4 cup of mirin (sweet cooking wine)
- 2 tbsp brown sugar

For the Finishing Touches:

- 1/4 cup of toasted sesame seeds
- 1/4 cup of chopped toasted almonds
- 1 head broccoli, cut into florets

Instructions

1. Put the chicken strips in a bowl and season with salt and pepper.
2. Mix the brown sugar, rice vinegar, honey, garlic, and ginger with a whisk in a small saucepan. Over medium flame, bring to a simmer and bake for 5 minutes, until it gets a little thicker.
3. Set your steamer basket over low heat and add water. Set the basket on top of the chicken strips and steam them for 5 to 7 minutes. On top of the chicken, add the broccoli florets. Steam for another 7 to 8 minutes or until the broccoli is soft but still crisp.
4. Place the broccoli and chicken on a serving platter. Add the teriyaki glaze and mix it in. To make it taste and look better, add sesame seeds and toasted almonds on top. Enjoy teriyaki with a nice crunch, the classic mix of sweet and savory flavors.

69. THAI FUSION BLISS WITH SWEET CHILI

Prep Time: 15 minutes | Cook Time: 15-20 minutes

Total Time: 30-35 minutes

Servings: 4-6

Ingredients

For the Vegetables:

- 1/2 cup of snap peas
- 1 red bell pepper, sliced
- 1 head broccoli, cut into florets
- 1 yellow bell pepper, sliced
- 1/2 cup of sliced bamboo shoots (optional)

For the Tofu:

- 1 tbsp cornstarch
- 14 ounce extra firm tofu, drained and pressed
- 1 tbsp olive oil
- 1/4 tsp black pepper
- 1/2 tsp salt

For the Peanut Sauce:

- 2 tbsp soy sauce
- 1/4 cup of coconut milk (optional, for a creamier sauce)
- 1 tbsp rice vinegar
- 1 tsp honey
- 1 tbsp water
- 1/2 tsp crushed red pepper flakes (adjust to your spice preference)
- 1/3 cup of smooth peanut butter
- 1 tsp lime juice

For the Garnish:

- Chopped fresh cilantro
- Roasted peanuts (optional)
- Lime wedges (optional)

Instructions

1. Set your steamer basket over low heat and add water. Put the snap peas, bell pepper slices, and broccoli florets in the basket. Steam for 5 to 7 minutes with the lid on. You should add the bamboo shoots in the last two minutes of steaming if you are using them.
2. Take the tofu and cut it into cubes while the vegetables steam. In a bowl, mix them with cornstarch, salt, and pepper.
3. Set the pan on medium flame and add the olive oil. Add the tofu cubes and cook, flipping every so often, until all sides are golden brown and crispy.
4. Mix the peanut butter, soy sauce, rice vinegar, water, lime juice, honey, and crushed red pepper flakes together in a small bowl using a whisk. If you want it to be creamier, add the coconut milk.
5. The steamed vegetables and cooked tofu should be split up between bowls. Add the peanut sauce and top with chopped cilantro, lime wedges (if you want), and roasted peanuts (if you want). Enjoy the tasty mix of sweet chili, smooth peanut sauce, and bright vegetables!

70. SAVORY MEATLOAF WITH HERB GLAZE

Prep Time: 15 minutes | Cook Time: 45-50 minutes

Total Time: 60-65 minutes

Servings: 6-8

Ingredients

For the Meatloaf:

- 1/4 cup finely chopped onion
- 1/2 cup breadcrumbs (fresh or panko)
- 1/4 cup grated Parmesan cheese
- 1 tablespoon Dijon mustard
- 1/2 teaspoon dried oregano
- 1 egg, beaten
- 1 tablespoon Worcestershire sauce
- 1 teaspoon dried thyme
- 1/4 cup finely chopped celery
- 1 pound lean ground beef (90/10 or turkey meat for lighter option)
- 1/4 teaspoon garlic powder
- Salt and freshly ground black pepper, to taste

Optional:

- 1/2 teaspoon smoked paprika
- 1/4 cup chopped walnuts or pecans
- 1/4 cup chopped sun-dried tomatoes
- 1/2 cup chopped mushrooms

Instructions

1. Get your electric steamer ready to go. Add the onion, celery, Dijon mustard, Worcestershire sauce, egg, thyme, oregano, garlic powder, salt, and pepper to a large bowl. Then add the ground meat and mix it all together. Make sure that all the ingredients are spread out evenly by mixing the mixture well.
2. Make an oval loaf out of the meatloaf mix on a plate or piece of parchment paper that can be used for steaming. You can make a shallow depression in the top of the loaf if you want to use it for basting with sauce later.
3. Place the shaped meatloaf in a steamer basket that has been lined with parchment paper. Put the lid on top and steam for 45 to 50 minutes, or until the food reaches 160°F (71°C) inside.
4. If you want, you can make a simple glaze while the meatloaf is steaming. Put 1/4 cup of ketchup, 1 tablespoon of brown sugar, and 1 teaspoon of Dijon mustard in a small saucepan. Keep heating on low until it gets a little thicker.
5. Before putting the meatloaf on a cutting board, let it cool a bit in the steamer. Apply the glaze if you're using it, and then cut the cake into pieces to serve. Elevator Savory Meatloaf tastes great with mashed potatoes, roasted vegetables, or a side salad.

71. PROVENCAL SUNSHINE WITH CREAMY COCONUT

Prep Time: 15 minutes | Cook Time: 15-20 minutes

Total Time: 30-35 minutes

Servings: 4

Ingredients

For the Salmon:

- Salt and pepper to taste
- 1 tbsp olive oil
- 4 salmon fillets (6 ounce each)

For the Mango Salsa:

- 1 ripe mango, diced
- 1/4 cup of red onion, finely chopped
- 1/2 tsp honey
- 1 jalapeno, seeded and finely chopped (adjust to spice preference)
- 1 tbsp chopped fresh cilantro
- 1 tbsp lime juice
- Pinch of salt and pepper
- 1/2 red bell pepper, diced

For the Creamy Coconut Sauce:

- 1 clove garlic, minced
- 1 tbsp Greek yogurt
- 1/4 cup of unsweetened coconut milk
- Salt and pepper to taste
- 1/2 tsp dried thyme

Instructions

1. Prepare the Salmon: Add salt and pepper to the salmon fillets. Put the olive oil and set it aside.
2. How to Make Mango Salsa: Put the Jalapeno, cilantro, lime juice, honey, salt, and pepper in a bowl. Add the mango, bell pepper, red onion, and hot pepper. Place aside to let the taste mix.
3. Get the coconut sauce ready: A small bowl holds the Greek yogurt, garlic, thyme, salt, and pepper. It is mixed with a whisk.
4. To steam the salmon, put water in the steamer basket and heat it until it just starts to simmer. Cover the salmon fillets in the basket. Salmon should be steamed for 15 to 20 minutes or until it's fully cooked and flaky when pierced with a fork.
5. Put together and serve: Put the smooth coconut sauce on plates. Add the steamed salmon and a big scoop of mango salsa on top. Enjoy the bright flavors and different textures of the fresh salsa, creamy sauce, and tender salmon!

72. MEDITERRANEAN DELIGHT WITH SUN-DRIED TOMATOES

Prep Time: 10 minutes | Cook Time: 15-20 minutes

Total Time: 25-30 minutes

Servings: 4

Ingredients

For the Salmon:

- 1 tbsp olive oil
- Salt and pepper to taste
- 4 salmon fillets (5 ounce each)

For the Sauce:

- 1 tbsp lemon juice
- 2 cloves garlic, minced
- 1/4 cup of sun-dried tomatoes, oil-packed and chopped
- 1/4 cup of chopped fresh parsley
- 1/4 cup of olive oil
- 1/4 cup of Kalamata olives, pitted and sliced
- 1/4 cup of chopped fresh basil
- 1/4 cup of dry white wine (optional)
- Salt and pepper to taste

Instructions

1. Set your steamer basket on high heat and add just enough water to cover it.
2. Sprinkle salt and pepper on the salmon. Put the olive oil on top and leave it alone.
3. Set the olive oil in a small pan and heat it over medium-low heat. Put in the garlic and bake for 30 seconds, until it smells good.
4. If you're using white wine, add it now and let it cook for one minute.
5. Add the olives, sun-dried tomatoes, basil, lemon juice, and parsley. Add pepper and salt to taste.
6. Cover the steamer basket and put the salmon fillets in it. Salmon should be steamed for 15 to 20 minutes or until it's fully cooked and flaky when pierced with a fork. Put the sauce on top of the steamed salmon and serve.

73. THAI CURRY WITH VEGETABLES AND TOFU

Prep Time: 15 minutes | Cook Time: 20-25 minutes

Total Time: 35-40 minutes

Servings: 4

Ingredients

For the Steaming:

- 1/2 cup of snap peas
- 1 yellow bell pepper, sliced
- 14 ounce extra firm tofu, drained and pressed, cubed
- 1 red bell pepper, sliced
- 1 head broccoli, cut into florets

For the Thai Curry:

- 1 tbsp soy sauce
- 1 (14 ounce) can light coconut milk
- 1 tbsp chopped fresh cilantro
- 2 tbsp red Thai curry paste (adjust to spice preference)
- 1 tbsp vegetable oil
- 1/2 cup of vegetable broth
- 1 tbsp brown sugar
- 1 onion, chopped
- 1 tbsp grated ginger
- 1 tbsp lime juice
- 2 cloves garlic, minced
- 1/2 tsp sriracha (optional)

For Serving:

- Cooked brown rice or quinoa
- Lime wedges (optional)
- Fresh cilantro sprigs (optional)

Instructions

1. Add water to your steamer basket and bring it to a simmer. Then add the vegetables and tofu and steam them. Put the bell pepper slices, snap peas, broccoli florets, and tofu cubes in the basket. Then, cover it. Steam the vegetables for 15-20 minutes, or until they are soft but still crisp and the tofu is warm all the way through.
2. Make the Thai curry. Put the oil in a large saucepan and heat it over medium-low heat while the vegetables and tofu steam. After you add the onion, cook for about 5 minutes or until it gets soft. After you add the garlic and ginger, cook for one more minute or until the food smells good.
3. Put the red Thai curry paste and stir it in. Cook for one minute, pulling up any browned bits from the pan's bottom.
4. Soy sauce, lime juice, brown sugar, and coconut milk should all be added. Bring to a simmer, then bake for 5 minutes while stirring every now and then.
5. Add the tofu and vegetables that have been steamed to the curry sauce. Heat it through for two to three minutes.
6. Add the chopped cilantro and sriracha (if using), and taste to see if the seasonings need to be changed.
7. Thai curry should be served with hot brown rice or quinoa. You can add lime wedges and fresh cilantro on top, but it's not necessary.

74. CHICKEN POT PIE WITH PUFF PASTRY CRUST

Prep Time: 15 minutes | Cook Time: 15-20 minutes

Total Time: 30-35 minutes

Servings: 4-6

Ingredients

For the Filling:

- 1/4 cup of cornstarch
- 2 carrots, chopped
- 2 cloves garlic, minced
- 1/2 cup of chicken broth
- 1/4 tsp dried rosemary
- 2 stalks celery, chopped
- 1 pound boneless, skinless chicken breasts, cooked and cubed
- 1 tbsp olive oil
- 1 (14.5 ounce) can diced tomatoes, undrained
- 1/2 tsp dried thyme
- Salt and pepper to taste
- 1 onion, chopped
- 1/2 cup of frozen peas

For the Puff Pastry Crust:

- 1 sheet frozen puff pastry, thawed

For Finishing Touches:

- 1 egg yolk, beaten with 1 tbsp water (egg wash)

Instructions

1. Put the olive oil in a large saucepan and heat it over medium-low heat. After you add the onion, cook for about 5 minutes or until it gets soft. After you add the garlic and celery, cook for one more minute or until the food smells good.
2. The carrots should be cooked for 5 to 7 minutes or until they get soft. Pour in the chicken broth, cornstarch, thyme, rosemary, salt, and pepper. Then add the frozen peas, diced tomatoes with their juices, and the cooked chicken. Bring to a low boil, then cook for 5 minutes or until it gets thick.
3. Put the pies together: Set your steamer basket on high heat and add just enough water to cover it. The filling should be split evenly between four ramekins or a large casserole dish.
4. Spread the puff pastry sheet out on a lightly floured surface to thaw. Make four circles that are bigger than the ramekins or casserole dish's diameter.
5. Use egg wash to cover the edges of the ramekins or dish. Carefully place the circles of puff pastry on top of the filling and press the edges together to seal. For a golden crust, brush egg wash on top.
6. To steam the pies, put the dish or ramekins in the steamer basket and cover them. The puff pastry should be golden brown and cooked all the way through after 15 to 20 minutes of steaming.
7. Wait a minute or two before serving the pies. With the help of your electric steamer, making this warm and comforting chicken pot pie was even easier.

75. MOROCCAN CHICKEN TAGINE WITH COUSCOUS

Prep Time: 15 minutes | Cook Time: 20-25 minutes

Total Time: 35-40 minutes

Servings: 4-6

Ingredients

For the Tagine:

- Pinch of saffron threads (optional)
- 1 (14.5 ounce) can diced tomatoes,
- 2 cloves garlic, minced
- 1/4 tsp ground cumin
- 1 tbsp olive oil
- 1/2 cup of chicken broth
- 1/4 cup of golden raisins
- 1/4 cup of dried apricots, chopped
- 1/2 tsp ground cinnamon
- 1 onion, chopped
- 1 inch fresh ginger, grated
- 1 pound boneless, skinless chicken thighs,
- 1/4 tsp paprika
- 1/2 tsp ground turmeric
- 1/4 cup of shelled almonds, toasted and chopped (optional)
- Fresh cilantro leaves, for garnish (optional)

For the Couscous:

- 1 1/4 cup of boiling water
- 1 tbsp olive oil
- Pinch of salt
- 1 cup of couscous

Instructions

1. Set up the tagine: In a large saucepan or Dutch oven that can fit your steamer basket, heat the olive oil. Put in the onion and cook for about 5 minutes, until it gets soft. The garlic, ginger, turmeric, cinnamon, cumin, paprika, and saffron (if using) should all be mixed in. Once it smells good, cook for one minute.
2. Add the chicken pieces and bake them all the way through until they are brown.
3. The chicken broth, apricots, raisins, and almonds (if using) should be added along with the diced tomatoes and their juices. Turn the heat down to low, cover, and move the pan to the electric steamer basket.
4. Bring the tagine to a boil: Put the lid on top of the steamer and steam for 20 to 25 minutes, or until the chicken is done and the sauce has become a little thicker.
5. Get the couscous ready by Putting the couscous and salt in a heat-safe bowl and mixing them together while the tagine steams. Pour the hot water over the couscous and tighten the lid. After 5 minutes, use a fork and a drizzle of olive oil to fluff the rice.
6. Gather and Serve: Put some couscous on each plate and then add some Moroccan Chicken Tagine on top of it. Add fresh cilantro leaves as a garnish if you want, and enjoy the wonderful mix of smells and textures!

76. SHRIMP AND VEGETABLE SPRING ROLLS

Prep Time: 20 minutes | Cook Time: 15-20 minutes

Total Time: 35-40 minutes

Servings: 12-16 spring rolls

Ingredients

For the Spring Rolls:

- 1/4 cup of chopped fresh mint
- 1 cup of warm water
- 1/2 pound cooked shrimp, peeled and deveined
- 12-16 round rice paper wrappers
- 1/4 cup of chopped fresh cilantro
- 1/2 cup of shredded cucumber
- 1/2 cup of bean sprouts
- 1/2 cup of shredded carrots
- Handful of romaine lettuce leaves

For the Dipping Sauce:

- 1 tbsp toasted sesame oil
- 1/4 cup of rice vinegar
- 1/4 cup of soy sauce
- 1/4 cup of water
- 1 clove garlic, minced
- 1 tbsp honey
- 1 inch fresh ginger, grated
- 1/2 cup of peanut butter
- Pinch of sriracha (optional)
- Lime wedges, for serving (optional)

Instructions

1. To make the filling, put the cooked shrimp, cucumber, bean sprouts, mint, cilantro, and lettuce leaves in a bowl and shred the carrots. Put away.
2. Get the dipping sauce ready by: For the peanut butter, soy sauce, honey, sesame oil, garlic, ginger, water, and sriracha (if using), mix them together in a small bowl using a whisk. If you need to, add more water to change the consistency. Put away.
3. Make the Spring Rolls: Put some warm water in a small bowl. For 10 to 15 seconds, soak one rice paper wrapper in water until it gets soft but not too bendy. With care, take the box off and lay it flat on a clean surface.
4. In the middle of the wrapper, close to the bottom edge, make a small mound of the filling. Add some shrimp on top. Turn the wrapper over so that the bottom edge is on top of the filling. Next, fold the sides in and roll it up tightly, like a burrito. Do it again with the rest of the filling and wrappers.
5. Place the spring rolls in a steamer basket and add just enough water to cover the rolls. Carefully move the spring rolls from the plate or steam tray to the steamer basket after putting them together. Put the lid on top and steam for 15 to 20 minutes, or until the wrappers are clear and the filling is hot all the way through.
6. Serve and Have Fun: Put the steamed spring rolls on a platter to serve. Serve it with lime wedges and the dipping sauce. These homemade spring rolls have bright flavors and light textures that you will love.

77. MEDITERRANEAN SUN-KISSED CHICKEN

Prep Time: 15 minutes | Cook Time: 25 minutes

Total Time: 40 minutes

Servings: 4

Ingredients

For the Chicken:

- 4 boneless, skinless chicken breasts
- 1 tbsp olive oil
- 1/2 tsp dried thyme
- 1/4 tsp ground cumin
- 1/2 tsp dried oregano
- Salt and pepper to taste

For the Vegetables:

- 1 yellow bell pepper, sliced
- 1 red onion, sliced
- 1 cup of cherry tomatoes
- 1 red bell pepper, sliced
- 1 zucchini, sliced

For the Grain:

- 1 1/4 cup of vegetable broth
- 1 cup of quinoa, rinsed
- 1/4 tsp dried thyme

For Serving:

- Fresh parsley, chopped (optional)
- Lemon wedges (optional)

Instructions

1. Set your steamer basket on high heat and add just enough water to cover it.
2. Mix olive oil, oregano, thyme, cumin, salt, and pepper in a small bowl. Add the chicken and mix it around. The chicken breasts or thighs should be rubbed with the mixture.
3. Plants should be roasted: Sprinkle the bell pepper, onion, zucchini, and cherry tomatoes with salt and olive oil. As they get soft and a little browned, put them on a baking sheet and roast them in an oven set to 400°F for 15 to 20 minutes.
4. Rinse the quinoa and put it, vegetable broth, and thyme in a saucepan. Put this aside while you roast the vegetables. Bring it to a boil, then turn down the heat and let it cook for 15 minutes or until the quinoa is fluffy and fully cooked.
5. To steam the chicken, put the chicken that has been marinated in a steamer basket and cover it. Steam the chicken for 15-20 minutes or until it's fully cooked and the juices run clear.
6. Put together and serve: Place the cooked quinoa on each plate. A sprinkle of fresh parsley is nice on top of the steamed chicken and roasted vegetables. Offer with lemon wedges for a zesty squeeze.

78. VEGETABLE LASAGNA WITH RICOTTA

Prep Time: 30 minutes | Cook Time: 30-35 minutes

Total Time: 1 hour 5-10 minutes

Servings: 4-6

Ingredients

For the Vegetables:

- 1 cup of broccoli florets
- 1 red onion, sliced
- 1 tbsp olive oil
- Salt and pepper to taste
- 1 medium zucchini, sliced
- 1/2 yellow bell pepper, sliced
- 1/2 red bell pepper, sliced

For the Ricotta and Spinach Filling:

- 1/4 tsp dried thyme
- 1 egg, beaten
- 1/4 tsp dried oregano
- 15 ounce ricotta cheese
- 1/4 cup of grated Parmesan cheese
- 1/2 cup of chopped fresh spinach
- Pinch of nutmeg
- Salt and pepper to taste

For the Lasagna:

- 1/4 cup of water
- 1 cup of shredded mozzarella cheese
- 1 tbsp olive oil
- 12 lasagna sheets (no-boil recommended)
- 1 (28 ounce) can crushed tomatoes
- 1/2 cup of chopped fresh basil

Instructions

1. Warm up your steamer basket with just enough water to make it simmer.
2. Get the vegetables ready: Salt and pepper should be added to the broccoli, bell peppers, onion, and zucchini. Put them on a baking sheet and roast them in an oven set to 400°F for 15 to 20 minutes. This will make them soft and crispy.
3. Compose the spinach and ricotta filling: Put spinach, ricotta cheese, Parmesan cheese, egg, oregano, thyme, nutmeg, salt, and pepper in a bowl. Thoroughly mix until everything is well combined.
4. How to put together the lasagna: Fill a baking dish that can hold your steamer basket with a thin layer of crushed tomatoes. Another layer of lasagna sheets on top.
5. Next, put a layer of roasted vegetables on top of the ricotta and spinach filling. Continue layering until all the ingredients are used up. Put a layer of pasta on top to finish.
6. In a bowl, mix the rested tomatoes that have been crushed with the basil, water, and olive oil. Pour the mixture on top of the lasagna's layers.
7. Toss the baking dish in the steamer basket and cover it with foil. Lasagna should be bubbling and hot after 30 to 35 minutes of steaming.
8. Remove the foil and add shredded mozzarella cheese on top. The cheese should be melted and golden brown after 5 to 7 minutes back in the steamer.
9. Prior to cutting and serving, let the lasagna cool for ten minutes. Enjoy this healthy and tasty vegetable lasagna's bright flavors and smooth textures!

79. SPICY CAJUN SHRIMP BOIL WITH CORN AND POTATOES

Prep Time: 15 minutes | Cook Time: 20-25 minutes

Total Time: 40 minutes

Servings: 4-6

Ingredients

For the Boil:

- 4 cups of chicken broth
- 1/2 tsp smoked paprika
- 1 onion, chopped
- 1 pound peeled and deveined shrimp
- 1/2 cup of Cajun seasoning blend
- 4 ears of corn, cut into thirds
- Fresh parsley, chopped (optional)
- 1 tsp dried thyme
- 1/4 tsp cayenne pepper (adjust to your spice preference)
- 1 tbsp olive oil
- 1/4 tsp black pepper
- 2 cloves garlic, minced
- 1 (14.5 ounce) can diced tomatoes, undrained
- 2 medium potatoes, diced
- Cooked rice or cornbread, for serving (optional)

Instructions

1. Just enough water should be in the basket of your electric steamer for it to simmer. Get the other things ready while it heats up.
2. Set your steamer basket inside a large saucepan or Dutch oven that can hold the olive oil. Heat the oil. After you add the onion, cook for about 5 minutes or until it gets soft. Add the paprika, cayenne pepper, black pepper, and Cajun seasoning blend and mix them well. Give the spices one more minute to bloom and give off their scent.
3. Get sexy: Add the chicken broth and the diced tomatoes with their juices. Bring it down to low heat and let it bubble for five minutes.
4. The star of the show is now going! Place the shrimp in the broth after they have been peeled and deveined. Add the shrimp and stir them slowly. Cook for 3–4 minutes or until they are just pink and opaque.
5. Add the diced potatoes and corn. Put the lid on the pot and move it to the steamer basket. Let it steam for 10 to 12 minutes or until the corn is fully cooked and the potatoes are soft.
6. Big Flavor, Easy Serve: Take the pot off the heat and stir the boil one last time. If you want, you can sprinkle chopped parsley on top and serve it piping hot with cornbread or cooked rice for a truly satisfying feast.

80. FLUFFY WHITE STEAMED BUNS

Prep Time: 15 minutes | Cook Time: 15-20 minutes

Total Time: 30-35 minutes

Servings: 8-10 buns

Ingredients

For the Dough:

- 1/4 cup of granulated sugar
- 1 1/4 tsp active dry yeast
- 1 tbsp vegetable oil
- 1/4 tsp salt
- 1 1/2 cups of all-purpose flour
- 1/4 cup of lukewarm milk

For Steaming:

- Water
- Parchment paper

Instructions

1. Add the yeast to a small bowl with warm milk and sugar. Mix them together to get the yeast going. Wait five to ten minutes or until the yeast starts to work and foam.
2. Mix the salt and flour together in a large bowl to make the dough. Put in the vegetable oil and the mix of activated yeast. Mix the stuff together little by little until a dough forms. Cover a work area with flour. Knead the dough for 5-7 minutes or until it is smooth and stretchy.
3. Rise and Shine: Grease a bowl and put the dough in it. Then, cover it tightly. Leave it somewhere warm for an hour or two so that it can double in size.
4. Making the Buns: Flatten the dough with your fingers and cut it into 8–10 equal pieces. Flatten each piece into a ball.
5. To get ready to steam, put just enough water in the steamer basket to make it simmer. Place parchment paper inside the basket to make it easy to take out.
6. Place the buns on the prepared steamer basket, leaving space between them so they can rise. Place a tight lid on top and steam for 15 to 20 minutes or until the buns are fully cooked and puffed up.
7. Enjoy: Let the buns cool down a bit before you serve them. Feel free to eat them plain, fill them with your favorite sweet or savory foods, or dip them in sauces to make them taste even better.

INTERNATIONAL FLAVORS

81. VIETNAMESE BUN CHAY

Prep Time: 20 minutes | Cook Time: 20-25 minutes

Total Time: 40-45 minutes

Servings: 4-6

Ingredients

For the Tofu:

- 1 tbsp brown sugar
- 1 tbsp rice vinegar
- 1/2 inch fresh ginger, grated
- 1 clove garlic, minced
- Pinch of ground black pepper
- 1 tbsp vegetable oil
- 12 ounce extra firm tofu, drained and pressed
- 2 tbsp soy sauce

For the Steaming:

- 1-2 heads romaine lettuce, leaves separated and washed
- 1/2 cup of fresh herbs (mint, basil, cilantro)
- 1 cup of shredded carrots
- 1 cup of bean sprouts

For the Dipping Sauce:

- 2 tbsp lime juice
- 1/4 cup of nuoc cham (fish sauce)
- 1/4 cup of chopped red bell pepper
- 1/4 cup of chopped carrots
- 1/2 cup of warm water
- 1 tbsp sugar
- 1 clove garlic, minced
- 1/2 inch fresh ginger, grated

For Serving:

- 6-8 toasted banh mi rolls (Vietnamese baguettes)
- Sriracha (optional)

Instructions

1. To make the tofu, cut it into cubes that are easy to eat. Add rice vinegar, brown sugar, garlic, ginger, black pepper, soy sauce, and vegetable oil to a bowl. Mix them all together.

Put the tofu cubes into the sauce and make sure they are all covered. For a stronger taste, let it sit for at least 30 minutes or up to 12 hours.
2. Make the vegetable steam: Just enough water should be in the basket of your electric steamer for it to simmer. Within the basket, spread out the romaine lettuce, carrot shreds, and bean sprouts. Cover and steam for 5-7 minutes or until the leaves are soft but still crisp.
3. Put together the Bun Chay: Place the steamed lettuce on plates. Put fresh herbs, steamed vegetables, and marinated tofu on top of each other.
4. How to make the dipping sauce: Warm water, nuoc cham, lime juice, sugar, garlic, ginger, chopped carrots, and chopped red bell pepper should all be mixed together in a small bowl using a whisk. Have fun dipping the Bun Chay in the tasty sauce!
5. Enjoy and Serve: Toasted banh mi rolls should be cut in half, and the Bun Chay should be put inside. Extra dipping sauce can be added if you want. You can add a little Sriracha for an extra kick if you want to.

82. JAPANESE GYOZA WITH SESAME GINGER DIPPING SAUCE

Prep Time: 15 minutes | Cook Time: 20-25 minutes

Total Time: 35-40 minutes

Servings: 4-6

Ingredients

For the Gyoza Filling:

- 1/2 pound ground pork or chicken
- 1 package (30-32) round wonton wrappers
- 1/4 tsp garlic powder
- 1 tbsp soy sauce
- 1/2 cup of finely chopped napa cabbage
- 1/2 tsp grated ginger
- 1 tsp sesame oil
- Pinch of ground black pepper
- 1 tbsp sake (optional)
- 1 tbsp cornstarch
- 1/4 cup of chopped green onion

For Cooking:

- 1-2 tbsp vegetable oil

For the Sesame Ginger Dipping Sauce:

- 1 tsp honey
- 1 tbsp toasted sesame oil
- 1/4 cup of soy sauce
- 2 tbsp rice vinegar
- 1 tbsp chopped scallions
- 1/2 tsp grated ginger
- 1 tsp sesame seeds, toasted
- 1 clove garlic, minced

For Serving:

- Chopped fresh cilantro (optional)

Instructions

1. Put the cabbage, green onion, soy sauce, ginger, garlic powder, black pepper, sesame oil, and cornstarch in a large bowl. You can also add sake if you want. Mix well until everything is well mixed.
2. Place a wonton wrapper flat on a clean surface. In the middle, put a round tbsp of filling. Use water to clean the edges of the wrapper. To seal the wrapper, pinch the edges together and then fold it in half to make a crescent. Fill and wrap the rest of the cookies again.
3. In a big nonstick frying pan set over medium heat, put one to two tbsp of vegetable oil. Be careful when putting the gyoza in the pan, and leave space between them. Let them fry for two to three minutes or until the bottoms turn golden brown.
4. Fill the pan with 1/2 cup of water. Place a tight lid on top and steam for 5 to 7 minutes, or until the gyoza are fully cooked and the filling is juicy.
5. Put the soy sauce, rice vinegar, sesame oil, honey, ginger, garlic, and scallions in a small bowl and mix them together while the gyoza cooks. Mix everything together with a whisk.
6. Place the steamed gyoza on a platter to serve. Add chopped cilantro and sesame seeds as a garnish if you want. Warm it up and dip it in the sesame ginger sauce for a delicious taste explosion!

83. KOREAN JAPCHAE

Prep Time: 20 minutes | Cook Time: 20-25 minutes

Total Time: 40-45 minutes

Servings: 4-6

Ingredients

For the Noodles:

- 8 ounce Korean sweet potato noodles (japchae)
- Boiling water

For the Vegetables:

- 1/2 cup of julienned carrots
- 1/2 cup of julienned bell peppers (red, yellow, green)
- 1/2 cup of julienned spinach
- 1/4 cup of julienned onion
- 1 clove garlic, minced

For the Beef:

- 1 tbsp soy sauce
- 6 ounce lean ground beef (or substitute with tofu or mushrooms)
- Pinch of black pepper
- 1/2 tsp sesame oil

For the Sauce:

- 2 tbsp honey
- 1 tbsp brown sugar
- 1/4 cup of soy sauce
- 1 tbsp rice vinegar
- 1/4 cup of toasted sesame oil
- 1 tsp sesame seeds, toasted (optional)

For Serving:

- Sesame seeds, toasted (optional)
- Chopped scallions (optional)

Instructions

1. Boil water and pour it over the sweet potato noodles in a large bowl. Let it soak for 15 to 20 minutes or until it gets soft and al dente. Run cold water over the drain and rinse.
2. Just enough water should be in the basket of your electric steamer for it to simmer. Put the onion, bell pepper, spinach, carrots, and bell pepper in the basket for 5 to 7 minutes, or until crisp-tender, cover and steam.
3. Put a little oil in a pan and set it over medium-low heat while the vegetables steam. Put in the ground beef and cook it until it turns brown. Get rid of any extra fat. Add the black pepper, sesame oil, and soy sauce and mix well. Put away.
4. A small bowl holds soy sauce, sesame oil, honey, brown sugar, and rice vinegar. Use a whisk to mix them together.
5. Put the cooked noodles and steamed vegetables in a large bowl. Put in the sauce and the cooked beef. Mix everything together until it's all well mixed.
6. If you want, you can top the japchae with chopped scallions and toasted sesame seeds. Enjoy the wonderful mix of tastes and textures in this famous Korean dish while it's still warm.

84. THAI GREEN CURRY WITH COCONUT MILK

Prep Time: 20 minutes | Cook Time: 20-25 minutes

Total Time: 40-45 minutes

Servings: 4-6

Ingredients

For the Curry:

- 1 cup of vegetable broth
- 1 (14.5 ounce) can unsweetened coconut milk
- 1/2 cup of chopped green beans
- 2 tbsp olive oil
- 1 cup of baby spinach
- 1 bell pepper (red or yellow), sliced
- 2 tbsp Thai green curry paste
- 2 cloves garlic, minced
- 1/2 cup of broccoli florets
- 1 tbsp brown sugar
- 1 lime, juiced
- 1 tbsp finely chopped ginger
- Salt and pepper to taste

For Serving:

- Cooked brown rice or quinoa
- Fresh basil leaves, chopped (optional)
- Sriracha (optional)

Instructions

1. Make sure the olive oil is warm in a large pot or Dutch oven that has enough room for your steamer basket. Add the ginger and garlic, and bake for one minute. The food should smell good at this point.
2. After you add the Thai green curry paste and stir it in, cook for one more minute to let the spices release their smell. The coconut milk and vegetable broth should be added. Bring to a simmer and let it bubble for three to four minutes to let the flavors mix.
3. Put just enough water in your steamer basket to simmer while the broth cooks. Put the green beans, broccoli florets, and sliced bell pepper in the basket. For 5 to 7 minutes, or until tender-crisp, cover and steam.
4. After you add the baby spinach to the broth that is already simmering, give it a minute or two to wilt.
5. Include the brown sugar and lime juice. Depending on your taste, add pepper and salt.
6. Move the steamed vegetables slowly into the curry that is already cooking. Combine and heat through. Place the Thai Green Curry over cooked brown rice or quinoa in bowls. Optional: Add some sriracha and fresh basil leaves on top for an extra kick.

85. CHINESE STEAMED FISH WITH GINGER

Prep Time: 15 minutes | Cook Time: 10-15 minutes

Total Time: 25-30 minutes

Servings: 2-3

Ingredients

For the Fish:

- 1/2 tsp rice wine or Shaoxing wine (optional)
- 1/4 tsp white pepper
- 1 tbsp soy sauce
- 1 whole white fish (around 12 ounce), cleaned and scaled
- 1 tsp cornstarch
- 1/4 tsp salt

For the Aromatics:

- 1 tbsp cooking oil (optional)
- 3 scallions, cut into 2-inch segments
- 3 slices fresh ginger

For Serving:

- Light soy sauce (optional)
- Chopped cilantro (optional)

Instructions

1. For drying the fish, you can use a paper towel. Put cornstarch, salt, white pepper, soy sauce, and rice wine in a small bowl. Carefully cut the fish along its sides. Apply the mixture to the inside and outside of the fish. Soak it somewhere else for 10 minutes.
2. Just enough water should be in the basket of your electric steamer for it to simmer. On top of the water, put the ginger and scallion slices on a plate. Cover and steam for 5 minutes. The scent will fill the steam.
3. Spread a little cooking oil on the steamer basket if you're using it. Put the fish that has been marinated on top of the aromatics.
4. Put the lid on top of the steamer and steam the fish for 10-15 minutes or until it is opaque and cooked all the way through. The cooking time may change based on how thick the fish is.
5. Move the steamed fish carefully to a plate for serving. Add more scallions or cilantro as a garnish if you want to. If you want, you can serve it with a small bowl of light soy sauce to dip it in.

86. CHICKEN TIKKA MASALA

Prep Time: 20 minutes | Cook Time: 20-25 minutes

Total Time: 40-45 minutes

Servings: 2-3

Ingredients

For the Chicken:

- 1 pound boneless, skinless chicken breasts or thighs, cut into bite-sized pieces
- 1/2 tsp garam masala
- 1/4 tsp garlic powder
- 1/8 tsp cayenne pepper
- 1/4 tsp paprika
- 1/4 tsp ginger powder
- 1 tbsp plain yogurt
- 1/4 tsp ground coriander
- 1/2 tsp turmeric powder
- Salt and pepper to taste

For the Sauce:

- 1 tbsp vegetable oil
- 1/2 cup of water
- 1/2 tsp sugar
- 1 (14.5 ounce) can diced tomatoes, undrained
- 1 tbsp tomato paste
- 1/2 onion, chopped
- 1/4 tsp ground cumin
- 1 clove garlic, minced
- Cilantro, for garnish (optional)
- 1 tbsp heavy cream (optional)

Instructions

1. Add yogurt, coriander, ginger, garlic, paprika, cayenne pepper, salt, and pepper to a bowl. Add the turmeric and garam masala. Put the chicken pieces and toss them around to make sure they are evenly covered. Leave to sit for at least 30 minutes or overnight for a stronger flavor.
2. Add enough water to your electric steamer basket to make it simmer. In the basket, arrange the chicken pieces that have been marinated. It should be covered and steamed for 15 to 20 minutes or until it's done.
3. With the chicken steaming, heat the oil in a saucepan over medium-low heat. Put in the onion and cook for about 5 minutes, until it gets soft. For one more minute, add the garlic. Add the water, tomato paste, sugar, cumin, heavy cream (if you want), and diced tomatoes. Lower the heat and let it cook for 10 minutes so the flavors can mix.
4. Use a blender to blend the sauce until it is smooth. Bring the mixture back to the pan and add the cooked chicken. Put it on high heat for a few minutes.
5. If you want, you can add cilantro to the Chicken Tikka Masala before serving it with rice or steamed naan.

87. MOROCCAN CHICKEN TAGINE WITH COUSCOUS

Prep Time: 20 minutes | Cook Time: 40-45 minutes

Total Time: 60-65 minutes

Servings: 4-6

Ingredients

For the Chicken Tagine:

- 1/2 tsp salt
- 1/2 cup of chicken broth
- 1 pound boneless, skinless chicken thighs, cut into bite-sized pieces
- 1 tbsp olive oil
- 1/4 tsp black pepper
- 1/2 tsp cinnamon
- 1/4 tsp cayenne pepper (adjust to your spice preference)
- 1/4 tsp paprika
- 1/4 cup of golden raisins
- 2 cloves garlic, minced
- 1 tsp ground ginger
- 1 (14.5 ounce) can diced tomatoes, undrained
- 1 onion, chopped
- 1/4 cup of dried apricots
- 1/4 cup of green olives
- 1/2 tsp turmeric
- 1 lemon, thinly sliced
- Cilantro, for garnish (optional)

For the Couscous:

- 1 tbsp olive oil
- 1 cup of Israeli couscous
- Pinch of pepper
- 1/2 tsp salt
- 1 1/2 cups of boiling water

Instructions

Chicken Tagine:

1. Olive oil, onion, garlic, ginger, turmeric, cinnamon, paprika, cayenne pepper, salt, and black pepper should all be mixed together in a bowl with chicken pieces. Add toss to cover evenly. Let it sit for at least 30 minutes or overnight for a stronger flavor.
2. Just enough water should be in the basket of your electric steamer for it to simmer. Put the chicken pieces that have been marinated in the basket. Put the lid on top and steam for 20 to 25 minutes or until the food is fully cooked.
3. Preheat up a tbsp of olive oil in a big pot or Dutch oven that fits your steamer basket while the chicken cooks. After you add the rest of the chopped onion, cook for about 5 minutes or until the onion is soft.
4. Add the spices (cinnamon, paprika, cayenne pepper, and turmeric) and mix them in. Toast the spices for one minute to let their smell come out.
5. The chicken broth, apricots, raisins, olives, and lemon slices should all be added now. Turn the heat down to low and let it cook for 10 minutes so the flavors can mix.
6. Move the cooked chicken from the steamer basket to the sauce that is already cooking. Mix slowly to combine and heat all the way through. You can add cilantro as a garnish and serve with fluffy couscous.

Couscous:

1. The couscous, boiling water, olive oil, salt, and pepper should all be mixed together in a different bowl. Lock the lid on tightly and let the couscous sit for 5 minutes or until it gets fluffy.
2. With a fork, fluff up the couscous and serve it with the Moroccan Chicken Tagine.

88. TURKISH MANTI DUMPLINGS

Prep Time: 30 minutes | Cook Time: 20-25 minutes

Total Time: 50-55 minutes

Servings: 4-6

Ingredients

For the Manti Dough:

- 1/4 cup of lukewarm water
- 1 1/2 cups of all-purpose flour
- 1/2 tsp salt
- 1 tbsp olive oil (optional)

For the Meat Filling:

- 2 cloves garlic, minced
- 1/4 cup of finely chopped onion
- 1/4 tsp paprika
- Salt and pepper to taste
- 1/4 tsp ground cumin
- 1/2 tsp dried oregano
- 1/2 pound ground beef or lamb

For the Yogurt Garlic Sauce:

- 1 tbsp chopped fresh mint
- 1 cup of plain yogurt (full-fat or Greek yogurt recommended)
- 1 tbsp olive oil
- 2 cloves garlic, minced
- Salt and pepper to taste

For Assembly and Serving:

- Clarified butter (optional)
- Chopped fresh parsley (optional)
- Chili flakes (optional)

Instructions

1. Combine the flour and salt together in a large bowl. While kneading, slowly add the lukewarm water and olive oil (if using) until a smooth, elastic dough forms. Put the dish in the fridge with the lid on for at least 30 minutes.
2. Mix the ground meat, onion, garlic, oregano, paprika, cumin, salt, and pepper in a bowl while the dough rests. Make sure to mix well so that the flavors are spread out evenly.
3. Create four to six equal pieces of dough. Separate each piece into a thin layer, then cut it into rounds or squares. Put a small amount of filling in the middle of each piece of dough. Press the edges together to make small dumplings in the shape of a crescent.
4. Put parchment paper inside your electric steamer basket to keep things from sticking. Placing the manti in the basket with enough space between them to steam evenly is important. The dough should be fully cooked, and the filling should be hot after 20 to 25 minutes of steaming.
5. In a bowl, mix the yogurt, garlic, mint, olive oil, salt, and pepper while the manti steams. While whisking, make sure the mixture is smooth and creamy.
6. Place the steamed manti on a plate to serve. Put the yogurt garlic sauce on top, and you can add melted clarified butter, chili flakes, or chopped parsley if you want to. Enjoy these Turkish treats' delicate tastes and textures!

89. ETHIOPIAN VEGAN MISIR WAT STEW

Prep Time: 20 minutes | Cook Time: 40-45 minutes

Total Time: 60-65 minutes

Servings: 4-6

Ingredients

For the Vegan Misir Wat Stew:

- 1 inch fresh ginger, grated
- 1 tbsp berbere spice blend
- 2 cups of vegetable broth
- Salt and pepper to taste
- 1 Jalapeno pepper, finely chopped (adjust to your spice preference)
- 1 (14.5 ounce) can diced tomatoes, undrained
- 1/4 cup of chopped fresh cilantro
- 2 cloves garlic, minced
- 1 tbsp olive oil
- 1 cup of red lentils, rinsed and soaked for at least 30 minutes
- 1/2 cup of water (adjust for desired consistency)
- 1 onion, chopped

For the Steamed Injera:

- 1 cup of teff flour
- Pinch of salt
- 1/2 cup of lukewarm water

For Serving (optional):

- Avocado slices
- Chopped red onion
- Sliced Jalapenos
- Chopped tomatoes

Instructions:

Vegan Misir Wat Stew:

1. Set your steamer basket inside a large pot or Dutch oven that can hold the oil. Heat the oil over medium-low heat. After you add the onion, cook for about 5 minutes or until it gets soft.
2. Add the Jalapeno, garlic, and ginger and mix them in. Cook for one more minute to let the fragrant smells come out.
3. After you add the berbere spice mix, cook for one more minute to let the bright flavors come out.
4. Put the tomato chunks, vegetable broth, and water in the pot. Turn the heat down to low and cook for 10 minutes.
5. Put in the lentils that have been soaked and drained. Simmer for another 20 to 25 minutes or until the lentils are soft. To keep things from sticking, stir every so often.
6. Add the chopped cilantro to the lentils after they are fully cooked. Add pepper and salt to taste.

Steamed Injera:

1. Put teff flour, lukewarm water, and salt in a bowl and mix them together. Mix the ingredients together well until a smooth batter forms. Turn it over and let it rise in a warm spot for at least two hours or until it goes double in size.
2. Place baking paper inside the basket of your electric steamer. Turn on the heat and let the water in the steamer base simmer.
3. Spread out about 1/4 cup of batter on the parchment paper to make a thin circle. Put the lid on top and steam for 5 to 7 minutes, or until the edges are set and the middle is bubbly.
4. Make more injera pancakes with the rest of the batter. Put them on a plate and wait for them to finish steaming.

Assemble and Savor:

1. Put some of the colorful Vegan Misir Wat Stew on a plate.
2. Cut the steamed injera into small pieces and use them to scoop up the tasty stew.
3. No need to: Add chopped red onion, tomatoes, Jalapenos, avocado slices, and more to the top for different tastes and textures.
4. Enjoy how this authentic Ethiopian treat has a unique mix of tastes and textures.

90. LEBANESE STEAMED KIBBEH MEATBALLS

Prep Time: 25 minutes | Cook Time: 20-25 minutes

Total Time: 45-50 minutes

Servings: 4-6

Ingredients

For the Steamed Kibbeh Meatballs:

- 2 cloves garlic, minced
- 1 cup of fine bulgur wheat, rinsed
- 1/2 tsp allspice
- 1/2 cup of warm water
- 1/4 tsp cinnamon
- 1 pound ground lamb or beef
- Salt and pepper to taste
- 1/2 onion, finely chopped

For the Tahini Sauce:

- 1/4 cup of orange juice
- 1/2 cup of tahini paste
- 2 cloves garlic, minced
- 1/4 cup of lemon juice
- 1/2 cup of water (adjust for desired consistency)
- Salt and pepper to taste
- 1 tbsp olive oil

For Serving (optional):

- Cucumber slices
- Chopped fresh parsley
- Mint leaves
- Chopped tomatoes

Instructions

Steamed Kibbeh Meatballs:

1. Wash the bulgur wheat and put it in a bowl. Add the warm water. Soak it for 15 minutes or until it gets soft.
2. Soak the bulgur wheat and put it in a large bowl. Add the ground meat, onion, garlic, allspice, cinnamon, salt, and pepper. Mix well until everything is well mixed.
3. To keep the mixture from sticking, wet your hands and roll it into walnut-sized meatballs.
4. Place baking paper inside the basket of your electric steamer. Lay the meatballs out in the basket so that they steam evenly. Leave some space between them. Put the lid on top and steam for 20 to 25 minutes or until the food is fully cooked.

Tahini Sauce:

1. Creamy Fusion: In a blender or food processor, combine tahini paste, lemon juice, orange juice, garlic, olive oil, and water. Blend until smooth and creamy. Adjust the water consistency as needed.
2. Season and Savor: Season the Tahini Sauce with salt and pepper to taste.

Assemble and Enjoy:

1. Arrange the steamed kibbeh meatballs on a serving platter.
2. Pour the Tahini Sauce over the meatballs, or serve it on the side for dipping.
3. Garnish with chopped parsley, mint leaves, chopped tomatoes, and cucumber slices (optional).
4. Enjoy the unique flavor and texture of Lebanese Steamed Kibbeh Meatballs with the vibrant touch of Tahini Sauce!

91. ITALIAN STEAMED MUSSELS WITH WHITE WINE

Prep Time: 10 minutes | Cook Time: 15-20 minutes

Total Time: 25-30 minutes

Servings: 2-3

Ingredients

- 2 cloves garlic, minced
- 2 pounds live mussels, debearded and cleaned
- Crusty bread, for dipping (optional)
- 1 tbsp olive oil
- Salt and pepper to taste
- 1/4 tsp dried thyme
- 1/2 cup of dry white wine (pinot grigio, sauvignon blanc, or vermouth work well)
- 1/4 cup of chopped fresh parsley
- 1/4 cup of chicken broth
- Pinch of red pepper flakes (optional)

Instructions

1. Run cold water over the mussels and scrub them with a brush to get rid of any sand or grit. Throw away any that have shells that are cracked or don't close properly when tapped.
2. In a large pot or Dutch oven suitable for your steamer basket, heat olive oil over medium heat. Add the garlic and bake for about 30 seconds, until fragrant.
3. Pour in the white wine, chicken broth, parsley, thyme, and red pepper flakes (optional). Bring to a simmer and let it bubble for 2-3 minutes.
4. Fill your electric steamer basket with parchment paper (optional) to prevent sticking. Gently add the mussels to the simmering broth. Cover and steam for 15-20 minutes or until the mussels open completely.
5. Stir the mussels to ensure even cooking. Put salt and pepper to taste to the broth.
6. Transfer the mussels and broth to a serving bowl. Discard any mussels that remain closed. You can add more parsley as a garnish, and the wonderful broth should be served with crusty bread for dipping.

92. GREEK STUFFED GRAPE LEAVES

Prep Time: 30 minutes | Cook Time: 40-45 minutes

Total Time: 70-75 minutes

Servings: 4-6

Ingredients

For the Stuffed Grape Leaves:

- 1/4 cup of chopped fresh parsley
- 1 tbsp lemon juice
- 1/4 cup of chopped fresh mint
- 1 tbsp olive oil
- 1/4 cup of chopped fresh dill
- 2 cloves garlic, minced
- 1/2 cup of finely chopped onion
- 1/4 tsp salt
- 1 cup of long-grain white rice, rinsed
- 1 jar (14.5 ounce) grape leaves, brined, rinsed, and drained
- 1/2 tsp dried oregano
- 1/4 tsp black pepper

For the Lemon Dressing:

- 1/4 cup of olive oil
- 2 tbsp lemon juice
- 1/4 tsp dried oregano
- Pinch of salt
- 1 tbsp water
- 1 clove garlic, minced
- Pinch of black pepper

Instructions

1. Soak fresh grape leaves in warm water for at least 30 minutes to make them soft and bendable. Put the rice aside after washing it. Add the mint, olive oil, lemon juice, oregano, salt, and pepper to a large bowl. Then, add the onion and garlic. Combine well.
2. Lay a grape leaf out flat with the vein side down. Put a spoonful of the rice mix next to the leaf's stem. Fold the sides in, and then roll the stem end up tightly to cover the filling completely. Do it again with the rest of the leaves and filling.
3. Place baking paper inside the basket of your electric steamer. Pile the stuffed grape leaves on top of each other, leaving space between them so that they steam evenly. Put the lid on top and steam for 40 to 45 minutes, or until the leaves are soft and the rice is done. Put the oregano, salt, pepper, olive oil, lemon juice, and water in a small bowl. Mix them together. Wait for the leaves to steam. Place away.
4. Put the steamed grape leaves on a plate to serve. Let them cool down a bit before adding the lemon dressing. Add more fresh herbs if you want, and then enjoy these delicious Greek Stuffed Grape Leaves with your family and friends!

93. SPANISH STEAMED BACALAO WITH ROMESCO

Prep Time: 15 minutes | Cook Time: 10-15 minutes

Total Time: 25-30 minutes

Servings: 2-3

Ingredients

For the Bacalao:

- 1 pound dried salt cod (bacalao), desalted and cut into thick slices
- 1 tbsp olive oil

For the Romesco Sauce:

- 2 roasted red peppers
- 2-3 Roma tomatoes, roasted (optional)
- 1/4 cup of raw almonds (or substitute walnuts, hazelnuts, cashews)
- 1 tbsp smoked paprika
- 2 tbsp sherry vinegar
- 2 cloves garlic, minced
- Salt and pepper to taste
- 1/2 cup of olive oil

For Serving (optional):

- Roasted potatoes
- Chopped fresh parsley
- Steamed spinach

Instructions

1. If your bacalao still needs to take salt out of it, soak it in cold water for 48 hours and change the water every 8 hours. Once the bacalao slices are no longer salty, use paper towels to gently dry them.
2. Warm the oven up to 400°F (200°C) if you are going to roast vegetables. Put tomatoes and red peppers on a baking sheet and roast them for 20-25 minutes until they get soft and a little charred. Let it cool down a bit, and then peel the peppers if you want to.
3. Put roasted peppers, tomatoes (if you want), almonds, garlic, vinegar, paprika, olive oil, salt, and pepper in a blender or food processor. Mix until it's creamy and smooth. Make the seasonings taste better.
4. Place baking paper inside the basket of your electric steamer. Place the bacalao slices one on top of the other. Put the lid on top and steam for 10 to 15 minutes or until the food is almost done and opaque. Watch out to cook the fish sparingly, or it will get tough.
5. Place the steamed bacalao on plates to be served. Put the bright Romesco sauce on top of the fish. You can add chopped parsley as a garnish and serve with roasted potatoes, steamed spinach, or any other sides you like.

94. FRENCH BOUILLABAISSE

Prep Time: 20 minutes | Cook Time: 40-45 minutes

Total Time: 60-65 minutes

Servings: 4-6

Ingredients

For the Broth:

- 1 can (14.5 ounce) diced tomatoes, undrained
- 1/2 tsp saffron threads
- 1 fennel bulb, chopped
- 1 bay leaf
- 2 cloves garlic, minced
- 1 tbsp olive oil
- Salt and pepper to taste
- 1/4 cup of chopped basil
- 1/4 cup of chopped parsley
- 1 tsp dried thyme
- 1 onion, chopped
- 6 cups of fish broth

For the Seafood:

- 1 pound mussels, debearded and cleaned
- 1 pound white fish fillets (cod, halibut, or sea bass work well), cut into bite-sized pieces
- Rouille (garlic mayonnaise), for serving (optional)
- 1/4 pound scallops, cleaned and patted dry
- Baguette slices, for serving (optional)
- 1/2 pound large shrimp, peeled and deveined

Instructions

1. Set your steamer basket inside a large pot or Dutch oven that can hold the oil. Heat the oil over medium-low heat. After you add the onion, cook for about 5 minutes or until it gets soft. The thyme, bay leaf, parsley, basil, and garlic should all be mixed in. For one more minute, cook until the fragrant smells come out.
2. Add the saffron threads, salt, pepper, and tomato chunks to the fish broth and mix them together. After you heat it up, let it sit for 10 minutes so the flavors can mix.
3. While the broth is cooking, get the seafood ready. Anything with an open shell should be thrown away. You should rinse and pat dry the fish, shrimp, and scallops.
4. Place baking paper inside the basket of your electric steamer. Stack the mussels one on top of the other, leaving space between them. Put a lid on them and steam them for 5 to 7 minutes or until their shells open all the way. Throw away any that are still closed.
5. Put the mussels that have been opened in a bowl and set it aside. Place the fish pieces in a single layer in the steamer basket. Put the lid on top and steam for 7 to 8 minutes or until the food is fully cooked and the color is clear. Take the fish out and put it somewhere else.
6. Put the scallops and shrimp in the steamer basket. Put the lid on top and steam for three to four more minutes or until the food is almost done. Watch out for cooking the shrimp and scallops too long, or they might get tough.
7. Put the cooked mussels, fish, and shellfish back into the broth. For about a minute or two, slowly heat through.
8. Place the bouillabaisse in bowls and offer rouille, crusty baguette slices for dipping, and a glass of crisp white wine. Enjoy the rich tastes and textures of this French treat!

95. GERMAN STEAMED DUMPLINGS WITH SAUERKRAUT

Prep Time: 30 minutes | Cook Time: 40-45 minutes

Total Time: 70-75 minutes

Servings: 4-6

Ingredients

For the Dumplings:

- 1 cup of all-purpose flour
- 1/4 tsp salt
- 1 tbsp butter, melted
- 1/2 cup of milk
- 1/2 tsp baking powder

For the Sauerkraut and Sausage Stew:

- 1 cup of chicken broth
- 1 (14.5 ounce) can sauerkraut, rinsed and drained
- 1 tbsp olive oil
- 2 cloves garlic, minced
- 1/2 pound smoked sausage (kiepoundasa, bratwurst, or weisswurst work well), sliced
- 1/4 tsp ground black pepper
- 1/2 tsp caraway seeds
- 1/2 cup of dry white wine (optional)
- 1 onion, chopped

For Serving (optional):

- Dijon mustard
- Chopped fresh parsley
- Sour cream

Instructions

1. Mix the flour, baking powder, and salt together in a large bowl using a whisk. Make a hole in the middle and add the milk and melted butter. Use a fork to mix slowly until a soft dough forms. Mix too much!
2. Place your steamer basket in a large pot or Dutch oven that can hold olive oil. Heat the oil. After you add the onion, cook for about 5 minutes or until it gets soft. Add the garlic and stir it in. Cook for 30 seconds or until it smells good.
3. Put in the black pepper, white wine (if you want), sauerkraut, and chicken broth. Bring it to a low boil, then let it cook for 15 minutes so the flavors can mix.
4. To make the sausage brown, put it in a separate pan and cook it until it's golden brown and fully cooked. Put away.
5. On a surface with a little flour, knead the dough a few times until it is smooth. Take small pieces of dough and roll them into balls that are about an inch across.
6. Place baking paper inside the basket of your electric steamer. Stack the dumplings one on top of the other, leaving space between them so that they steam evenly. Put the lid on top and steam for 15 to 20 minutes or until the dumplings are fluffy and fully cooked.
7. Put the sauerkraut stew in bowls to serve. Put the cooked sausage on top, then the fluffy steamed dumplings. If you want, you can sprinkle chopped parsley on top and serve with Dijon mustard and sour cream for dipping.

96. MEXICAN STEAMED TAMALES WITH CHICKEN

Prep Time: 40 minutes | Cook Time: 40-45 minutes

Total Time: 80-85 minutes

Servings: 10-12 tamales

Ingredients

For the Masa Dough:

- 1 tsp baking powder
- 1/2 tsp salt
- 1 1/2 cups of warm chicken broth
- 2 cups of masa harina (corn flour)
- 1/4 cup of water (adjust for desired consistency)
- 1/4 cup of vegetable shortening

For the Chicken Filling:

- 1 (14.5 ounce) can diced tomatoes, undrained
- 2 cloves garlic, minced
- 1 onion, chopped
- 1/4 tsp dried oregano
- 1 cup of cooked and shredded chicken
- 1 tbsp olive oil
- 1/2 cup of mole sauce (store-bought or homemade)
- Salt and pepper to taste
- 1/4 tsp ground cumin

For Serving (optional):

- Cotija cheese
- Chopped fresh cilantro
- Salsa
- Sliced avocado

Instructions

1. Do this for at least 30 minutes to soften the dried corn husks. Prior to using them, dry them off with a clean towel.
2. In a large bowl, use a whisk to mix the masa harina, baking powder, and salt together. Shortening should be rubbed into the dry ingredients until they look like coarse crumbs. Slowly add the warm chicken broth and water while mixing all the time until a soft dough forms. You should make a small change to the amount of water. Leave the dough alone for 20 minutes with the lid on.
3. Set a pan on medium flame and add the olive oil. After you add the onion, cook for about 5 minutes or until it gets soft. Add the garlic and stir it in. Cook for one more minute, letting the smell come out.
4. Add the chicken that has been cooked, the mole sauce, oregano, cumin, salt, and pepper. Let the flavors blend for 10 to 15 minutes while it simmers. Make the seasonings taste better.
5. Make a border at the top of the masa dough and spread it out thinly on a softened corn husk. Add some chicken filling to the bottom of the dough with a spoon. Fold the sides of the husk in toward the middle, and then roll it up from the bottom to cover the filling completely. Use string or a strip of corn husk to hold the end in place. Do it again with the rest of the dough and filling.
6. Place baking paper inside the basket of your electric steamer. Place the tamales on a flat surface, leaving space between them so that they steam evenly. Put the lid on top and steam for 40 to 45 minutes, or until the masa is fully cooked and the husks are easy to pull off.
7. Take the tamales out of the steamer carefully and let them cool down a bit before you serve them. If you want, you can add salsa, chopped cilantro, sliced avocado, and Cotija cheese as a garnish. Enjoy these tasty Steamed Tamales with Mole Sauce and Chicken!

97. BRAZILIAN MOQUECA DE PEIXE

Prep Time: 20 minutes | Cook Time: 30-35 minutes

Total Time: 50-55 minutes

Servings: 4-6

Ingredients

For the Fish:

- 1 tbsp lime juice
- 1/4 tsp black pepper
- 1/2 tsp salt
- 1 pound firm white fish fillets (cod, halibut, mahi-mahi, or tilapia work well), cut into bite-sized pieces

For the Broth:

- 1 (13.5 ounce) can unsweetened coconut milk
- 1 (14 ounce) can diced tomatoes, undrained
- 1 onion, chopped
- 1/4 cup of chopped fresh parsley
- Salt and pepper to taste
- Pinch of cayenne pepper (optional)
- 2 cloves garlic, minced
- 1 tbsp olive oil
- 1 tbsp dendê oil (palm oil, substitute vegetable oil if unavailable)
- 1/2 cup of chopped fresh cilantro
- 1/2 tsp ground cumin
- 1/4 tsp paprika
- 1 tsp dried oregano
- 1 green bell pepper, chopped (optional)
- 1 red bell pepper, chopped (optional)

For Serving (optional):

- Chopped fresh lime wedges
- Cooked white rice
- Coconut flakes

Instructions

1. Mix the fish pieces with salt, pepper, and lime juice in a bowl. While you make the broth, let them sit for at least 15 minutes.
2. Place your steamer basket in a large pot or Dutch oven that can hold olive oil. Heat the oil. After you add the onion, cook for about 5 minutes or until it gets soft. Add the garlic and stir it in. Cook for one more minute, letting the smell come out.
3. If you want to add bell peppers, chop them up and cook for 3 to 4 minutes until they start to get a little soft.
4. Put the chopped tomatoes, coconut milk, dendê oil, oregano, cumin, paprika, cayenne pepper (if you want), salt, and pepper into the pan. Heat it up, then let it sit for 5 minutes to let the flavors blend.
5. While the broth is cooking, put parchment paper in the basket of your electric steamer. Put the pieces of fish that have been marinated in a single layer. Put the lid on top and steam for 10 to 12 minutes or until the fish is opaque and cooked all the way through.
6. Add the cooked fish to the broth that is already simmering. For another minute or two, slowly heat through.
7. If you want, you can serve the Moqueca de Peixe hot overcooked white rice. Add coconut flakes and lime wedges as a garnish if you want to. Enjoy the bright tastes and textures of this Brazilian treat!

98. CUBAN ROPA VIEJA

Prep time: 20 minutes | Cook time: 40-45 minutes

Total time: 60-65 minutes

Servings: 4-6

Ingredients

For the Beef:

- 1/2 tsp dried oregano
- 1 tbsp olive oil
- 1 pound flank steak, trimmed and cut into 1-inch cubes
- 1/4 tsp black pepper
- 1/4 tsp salt
- 1/2 tsp ground cumin
- 1/4 tsp smoked paprika

For the Sauce:

- 2 cloves garlic, minced
- 1/4 tsp ground cumin
- 1/2 tsp dried oregano
- 1/2 cup of beef broth
- 1/4 tsp smoked paprika
- 1/4 cup of chopped fresh cilantro
- Salt and pepper to taste
- 1 onion, chopped
- 1 (14.5 ounce) can diced tomatoes, undrained
- 1 tbsp olive oil
- 1 tbsp red wine vinegar (optional)
- 1 (8 ounce) can tomato sauce
- Pinch of cayenne pepper (optional)

For Serving (optional):

- Sliced avocado
- Chopped fresh parsley
- Cooked white rice or black beans

Instructions

1. Add the beef cubes to a bowl and season with salt, pepper, oregano, cumin, and other spices. While you make the sauce, let the mixture sit for at least 15 minutes.
2. Place your steamer basket in a large pot or Dutch oven that can hold olive oil. Heat the oil. After you add the onion, cook for about 5 minutes or until it gets soft. Add the garlic and stir it in. Cook for one more minute, letting the smell come out.
3. Dice the tomatoes and add them to the pot. Then add the tomato sauce, beef broth, cilantro, oregano, cumin, paprika, cayenne pepper (if you want), salt, and pepper. Heat it up, then let it sit for 5 minutes to let the flavors blend.
4. Stack parchment paper in the basket of your electric steamer while the sauce cooks. Lay out the beef cubes that have been marinated in a single layer. Put the lid on top and steam for 20 to 25 minutes or until the beef is done and just a little soft.
5. Put the steamed beef on a cutting board and use two forks to shred it. You could also use a hand mixer with a dough hook attachment to shred the food faster.
6. Put the shredded beef back into the sauce that is already cooking. Warm it up slowly for another 5 to 7 minutes to let the flavors mix.
7. You can serve the Cuban Ropa Vieja hot on top of cooked black beans or white rice. You can add chopped fresh parsley and sliced avocado as a garnish. Have fun with this new take on a classic Cuban dish!

99. PERUVIAN STEAMED CEVICHE

Preparation Time: 20 minutes | Cooking Time: 10-15 minutes

Total Time: 30-35 minutes

Servings: 4-6

Ingredients

- 1/4 cup of chopped red onion
- 1 clove garlic, minced
- 1/2 cup of fresh lime juice
- 1/4 tsp black pepper
- 1/4 cup of fresh orange juice
- 1/2 tsp salt
- 1 pound firm white fish fillets
- 1/4 cup of chopped cilantro
- 1 Jalapeno pepper, seeded and finely chopped
- Pinch of ground cumin (optional)
- Pinch of smoked paprika (optional)
- Sweet potato slices or corn kernels, for serving (optional)

Instructions

1. Mix the orange juice, lime juice, red onion, cilantro, Jalapeno, garlic, salt, pepper, cumin (if you want), and paprika (if you want) in a large bowl. Mix it slowly and wait a few minutes so the flavors can mix.
2. Stir the fish slices into the citrus marinade while being careful not to break them up. Put the bowl in the fridge with the lid on for no more than 15 minutes to let the flavors blend. Too much marinade can make the fish tough.
3. You can put parchment paper or a lightly oiled banana leaf in the basket of your electric steamer. Place the fish pieces that have been marinated in a single layer. Put the lid on top and steam for 10 to 15 minutes or until the fish is opaque and fully cooked. Be careful not to cook it too long, or it will get dry.
4. Move the steamed ceviche to a platter or bowl for each person to serve. Be careful not to drown the fish when you pour the rest of the citrus marinade over it.
5. Add more chopped cilantro as a garnish and serve with roasted sweet potato slices or corn kernels as an alternative side dish. Enjoy the bright and delicate flavors of this ceviche steamed in an electric steamer!

100. ARGENTINIAN STEAMED EMPANADAS

Prep Time: 30 minutes | Cook Time: 30-35 minutes

Total Time: 60-65 minutes

Servings: 15-20 empanadas

Ingredients

For the Empanada Dough:

- 2 cups of all-purpose flour
- 1/4 cup of cold unsalted butter, cubed
- 1/4 cup of ice water
- 1 egg yolk, beaten (for egg wash)
- 1/2 tsp salt

For the Beef Filling:

- 1/2 tsp dried oregano
- 1 pound ground beef
- 1 tbsp olive oil
- 1/4 tsp ground cumin
- 1 (14.5 ounce) can diced tomatoes, undrained
- Salt and pepper to taste
- 1/2 cup of beef broth
- 2 cloves garlic, minced
- 1 onion, chopped
- 1/4 tsp paprika

For the Chimichurri:

- 1/4 tsp dried oregano
- 2 cloves garlic, minced
- 1/4 tsp red pepper flakes (adjust to your spice preference)
- 1/4 cup of chopped fresh cilantro
- 1/4 cup of red wine vinegar (optional, substitute lemon juice)
- 1/2 cup of chopped fresh parsley
- 1/4 cup of olive oil
- Salt and pepper to taste

Instructions

1. Combine flour and salt together in a big bowl. Cut the butter into cubes and mix them in with your fingers or a pastry cutter until the mixture looks like coarse crumbs. One tbsp at a time, add the ice water until a dough forms. Mix too much! For at least 30 minutes, put the dough in the fridge while it's wrapped in plastic wrap.
2. In a big pan, flame the olive oil over medium-low heat. After you add the onion, cook for about 5 minutes or until it gets soft. Add the garlic and stir it in. Cook for one more minute, letting the smell come out.
3. Put in the ground beef and cook it until it turns brown. The beef broth, oregano, cumin, paprika, salt, and pepper should all be stirred in now. Bring it to a simmer and let it cook for 15 to 20 minutes so the flavors can mix.
4. Get the chimichurri ready while the beef filling is simmering. Put chopped parsley, cilantro, garlic, oregano, red pepper flakes (if you want), olive oil, red wine vinegar (if you want), salt, and pepper in a small bowl. Mix well, then set it aside.
5. Warm up your electric steamer and put parchment paper inside the basket. To make the dough about 1/8-inch thick, roll it out on a lightly floured surface while it is still cold. Use a cookie cutter or a glass to make circles.
6. Put some of the cooled beef filling in the middle of each circle of dough. Spread the egg yolk around the edges. To seal the edges, fold the dough in half and press them together with a fork.
7. In the steamer basket, lay out the empanadas in a single layer. Put the lid on top and steam for 30-35 minutes or until the dough is golden brown and cooked all the way through.
8. Carefully take the empanadas out of the steamer and let them cool down a bit before serving. Add a drizzle of chimichurri sauce on top, and enjoy!

DESSERTS & SWEET ENDINGS

101. STEAMED APPLE CRUMBLE WITH VANILLA ICE CREAM

Prep Time: 20 minutes | Cook Time: 30-35 minutes

Total Time: 50-55 minutes

Servings: 4-6

Ingredients

For the Apples:

- 1/2 tsp ground cinnamon
- Pinch of salt
- 6-8 medium apples, peeled, cored, and thinly sliced
- 2 tbsp brown sugar
- 2 tbsp lemon juice
- 1/4 tsp ground nutmeg (optional)

For the Crumble Topping:

- 1/4 cup of brown sugar
- Pinch of salt
- 1/4 cup of cold unsalted butter, cubed
- 3/4 cup of rolled oats
- 1/2 cup of all-purpose flour
- 1/4 cup of chopped walnuts or pecans (optional)

For Serving (optional):

- Caramel sauce
- Vanilla ice cream
- Whipped cream

Instructions

1. Put the sliced apples, lemon juice, brown sugar, cinnamon, nutmeg (if you want), and salt in a large bowl. Spread the coating out by tossing. Give it ten minutes to sit so the flavors can blend.
2. Oats, flour, brown sugar, and salt should all be mixed together in a different bowl. Put the cubed butter and stir it in with your fingers or a pastry cutter until the mixture looks like coarse crumbs. If you want, you can add the chopped nuts now.
3. Insert parchment paper into the basket of your electric steamer. Spread the apple mix out evenly in the basket as you spoon it in. Really, make sure to cover all of the apples with the crumble topping.
4. Cover and steam for 30 to 35 minutes, or until the crumble topping is golden brown and the apples are soft.
5. Carefully take the crumble out of the steamer and let it cool down a bit before you serve it. Put a scoop of vanilla ice cream, whipped cream (if you want), and a drizzle of caramel sauce (if you want) into each bowl of warm crumble. Relax with this Steamed Apple Crumble!

102. TROPICAL FRUIT AND YOGURT PARFAIT

Prep Time: 15 minutes | Cook Time: 10-15 minutes

Total Time: 25-30 minutes

Servings: 4-6

Ingredients

For the Fruit:

- 1 kiwi, peeled and diced
- 1/2 cup of blueberries
- 1 pineapple, ripe and diced
- 1 mango, ripe and diced
- 1/4 cup of chopped fresh mint (optional)
- 1 tbsp brown sugar (optional)
- 1/4 tsp ground cinnamon (optional)

For the Yogurt:

- 2 cups of plain Greek yogurt
- 1/4 cup of honey or maple syrup

For Serving (optional):

- Granola or toasted coconut flakes
- Drizzle of honey or maple syrup

Instructions

1. Dice the mango, pineapple, kiwi, blueberries, and mint (if you want to add it). Put the fruit in a bowl. The fruits can be mixed together directly, or they can be layered in individual parfait glasses to make them look nicer.
2. If desired, The Steaming Delight: Putting parchment paper in your electric steamer basket will make the fruit a little softer and warmer. Separate the fruit into a single layer. Put the lid on top and steam for 10 to 15 minutes or until it's just warm. You don't have to do this step if you'd rather have a fresh and cool parfait.
3. If you want to, you can sprinkle the fruit with brown sugar and cinnamon and toss it to coat it. Leave it alone for a while so the flavors can mix.
4. Put the plain Greek yogurt and honey or maple syrup in a different bowl and mix them together. You can change how sweet it is to your liking.
5. Put the sweetened fruit mixture on top of the creamy yogurt in parfait glasses or bowls. Do this again and again until the glasses are full.
6. You can add granola or toasted coconut flakes to the top of your parfaits if you want to. Taste it and enjoy! If you want, add more honey or maple syrup.

103. STICKY RICE MANGO PUDDING WITH COCONUT CREAM

Prep Time: 15 minutes | Cook Time: 20-25 minutes

Total Time: 35-40 minutes

Servings: 4-6

Ingredients

For the Sticky Rice:

- 1 cup of glutinous rice (sweet rice)
- 1 1/2 cups of water
- 1/4 cup of white sugar
- 1/4 tsp salt
- 1 pandan leaf, knotted (optional)

For the Coconut Cream:

- 1 (13.5 ounce) can unsweetened coconut milk
- 1/4 cup of white sugar
- 1/4 tsp ground cardamom
- Pinch of salt

For Serving:

- 1 ripe mango, peeled and sliced
- Toasted coconut flakes (optional)

Instructions

1. Setting up the sticky rice: Use a fine-mesh strainer to wash the glutinous rice until the water runs clear. Remove the water and set it aside.
2. To steam the rice, put the washed rice, water, sugar, salt, and (if you want) a pandan leaf in the basket of your electric steamer. Place the lid on top and steam for 20 to 25 minutes or until the rice is fully cooked and has a few clear spots. If you'd like the rice to be fluffier, you can simmer it for 15 minutes in the same water and ingredients before steaming it.
3. Enjoy Coconut Cream Bliss! In a saucepan, mix the coconut milk, sugar, cardamom, and salt while the rice is steaming. Over medium flame, bring to a simmer, and stir every now and then. Let it cook on low heat for five minutes so the flavors can mix.
4. Sweet Reunion: Put the cooked sticky rice in a bowl for serving or into bowls for each person. Spread the warm coconut cream out evenly over the rice as you pour it on.
5. Put sliced mangoes on top of the creamy rice pudding for a tropical treat. Add toasted coconut flakes as a garnish if you want, and enjoy!

104. STEAMED BERRIES WITH HONEY AND MINT

Prep Time: 5 minutes | Cook Time: 10-15 minutes

Total Time: 15-20 minutes

Servings: 2-4

Ingredients

- 1/4 cup of fresh mint leaves, roughly chopped
- 1 cup of mixed berries (blueberries, raspberries, strawberries, etc.)
- 1 tbsp honey
- Optional: Lime zest, vanilla extract, or a sprinkle of powdered sugar

Instructions

1. Pick out a mix of fresh berries and wash and pat them dry briefly. Lay them out in a single layer in the basket of your electric steamer that has been lined with parchment paper.
2. Sprinkle the berries with a tbsp of honey so that they are just barely covered.
3. Add the chopped mint leaves to the berries that have been kissed with honey.
4. Cover the berries and steam them for 10-15 minutes, depending on how ripe they are and what texture you want. Try to get berries that are just warm and slightly softened but not mushy.
5. Serve the steamed berries to each person in a bowl or dish. You can add powdered sugar, a twist of lime zest, or a drop of vanilla extract to make the taste even better.
6. Enjoy the Steamed Berries with Honey and Mint, either warm or cold. The honey and mint add a subtle flavor to the berries, which are already naturally sweet.

105. POACHED PEACHES WITH VANILLA BEAN YOGURT

Prep Time: 10 minutes | Cook Time: 15-20 minutes

Total Time: 25-30 minutes

Servings: 4-6

Ingredients

For the Poached Peaches:

- 1/2 vanilla bean, split and scraped (or 1 tsp vanilla extract)
- 4 ripe peaches, halved and pitted
- 1/2 cup of white sugar
- 1 cup of water
- Pinch of ground cinnamon (optional)

For the Vanilla Bean Yogurt:

- 1/2 vanilla bean, split and scraped (or 1 tsp vanilla extract)
- 2 cups of plain Greek yogurt
- 1/4 cup of honey or maple syrup

For Serving (optional):

- Drizzle of honey or maple syrup
- Toasted nuts (almonds, pecans, pistachios)
- Fresh mint leaves

Instructions

1. Wash the peaches and cut them in half, taking out the pits. You can leave the skin on if you want to add more texture and nutrients.
2. Add the water, sugar, vanilla bean (scrape the seeds into the liquid), and cinnamon (if you want to) to the basket of your electric steamer. Put the sugar and stir to mix it.
3. Place the peach halves in the steamer basket so that the cut side is facing down. Put the lid on top and steam for 15-20 minutes, or until the peaches are soft and almost see-through but still have their shape.
4. In a different bowl, mix the plain Greek yogurt, honey or maple syrup, and vanilla bean (scrape out the seeds or use extract) while the peaches are steaming. You can change how sweet it is to your liking.
5. Place the yogurt in bowls or parfait glasses that can be used for serving. Add the poached peaches to each serving, either warm or cool, and drizzle with the syrup that came from the steaming basket.
6. Adding toasted nuts, fresh mint leaves and a drizzle of extra honey or maple syrup as a garnish is optional. Have fun with the light and refreshing Poached peaches cooked in a steamer with vanilla bean yogurt!

106. CHOCOLATE CHIP BANANA BREAD

Prep Time: 15 minutes | Cook Time: 40-45 minutes

Total Time: 55-60 minutes

Servings: 8-10 slices

Ingredients

Wet Ingredients:

- 1/4 cup of brown sugar
- 1 tsp vanilla extract
- 1 egg
- 1/2 cup of melted butter or coconut oil
- 2 ripe bananas, mashed

Dry Ingredients:

- 1 1/2 cups of all-purpose flour
- 1/2 tsp baking soda
- 1/2 cup of chocolate chips (milk, dark, or semi-sweet, as you prefer)
- 1/4 tsp salt

Optional Additions:

- 1/4 tsp ground cinnamon or nutmeg
- 1/2 cup of chopped nuts (walnuts, pecans, etc.)
- 1/4 cup of dried fruit (raisins, cranberries, etc.)

Instructions

1. Warm up your electric steamer and put parchment paper in a small loaf pan.
2. Mash the bananas in a big bowl until they are smooth. The melted coconut oil or butter, brown sugar, egg, and vanilla extract should all be mixed in well.
3. A different bowl should be used to mix the flour, baking soda, and salt. Mix this dry mix in slowly with the wet ones, stirring just until everything is mixed. Not too much mixing! Adding the chocolate chips and anything else you want is fine.
4. Fill the loaf pan with the batter once it's ready. Place a lid or foil over the pan to keep water from entering the batter. Insert the basket into the steamer and cover the pan. Take a toothpick and stick it in the middle. It should come out clean after 40 to 45 minutes.
5. After 10 minutes, move the bread to a wire rack to cool completely. Once it's cool, cut it up and start eating!

107. STEAMED MOLTEN LAVA CAKES

Prep Time: 10 minutes | Cook Time: 10-12 minutes

Total Time: 20-22 minutes

Servings: 4-6 cakes

Ingredients

- 2 large eggs, separated
- 4 tbsp unsalted butter, melted
- 4 ounces dark chocolate, chopped
- 2 tbsp granulated sugar
- 1/4 cup of all-purpose flour
- Pinch of salt
- Vanilla ice cream or whipped cream (optional)

Instructions

1. In a bowl that can go in the microwave or a double boiler, stir the chocolate and butter together. Mix the things together until the mixture is smooth and shiny. Wait a minute or two and let it cool down.
2. Different bowls should be used for the egg whites and yolks. Make the egg yolks fluffy and light by whisking them. Combine the chocolate and egg yolks carefully.
3. Put the flour and salt in a different bowl and mix them together. As you slowly add the dry mixture to the chocolate mixture, gently fold it in until it's all mixed together.
4. Lightly beat the egg whites in a clean bowl until they form stiff peaks. Put a third of the beaten egg whites into the chocolate batter at a time, being careful not to make the batter too heavy. Put in the rest of the egg whites after that.
5. Every ramekin or mug should be about three-quarters full of batter. Using parchment paper to line the steamer basket, put them in. For 10 to 12 minutes, or until the edges are set but the middle is still a little wobbly, put the lid on top and steam.
6. Allow the ramekins to cool for a while after slowly taking them out of the steamer. When the cakes cool down, they get even better.
7. You could put vanilla ice cream or whipped cream on top of the warm Steamed Molten Lava Cakes if you wanted to. You can cut a hole in the middle with a spoon to let the warm, gooey chocolate flow out. This makes an incredibly tasty dessert!

108. DARK CHOCOLATE STEAMED PUDDING

Prep Time: 20 minutes | Cook Time: 25-30 minutes

Total Time: 45-50 minutes

Servings: 4-6 puddings

Ingredients

For the Pudding:

- 2 tsp baking powder
- 1 tsp vanilla extract
- 100g unsalted butter, softened
- 100g caster sugar
- 50g cocoa powder
- 175g plain flour
- 100g dark chocolate (50% cocoa solids), melted
- 80g brown sugar
- 3 eggs
- 50ml cream

For the Raspberry Sauce:

- 2 tbsp golden syrup
- 250g fresh raspberries
- 180ml cream

Instructions

Pudding Perfection:

1. Warm up your electric steamer and grease your ramekins or pudding molds.
2. Softened butter and sugar should be mixed together with a hand mixer or stand mixer until the mixture is light and creamy.
3. One at a time, add the eggs and beat until everything is well-mixed. Then, put the vanilla extract and mix it in.
4. Mix the cocoa powder, baking powder, and flour together using a sieve. Slowly add this dry stir to the wet ones, mixing in the cream between each addition. Don't overmix; mix until everything is combined.
5. Mix the melted dark chocolate in slowly.
6. Spread the batter out evenly in the molds that have been prepared.

Steam the Delight:

1. Put the molds in the steamer basket that has been lined with parchment paper. Place a toothpick in the middle and cover. Steam for 25-30 minutes or until the toothpick comes out clean.

Raspberry Symphony:

1. The raspberry sauce should be made while the puddings are steaming. Put the cream, golden syrup, and fresh raspberries in a saucepan. Over medium-low heat, slowly bring the berries to a boil while mashing them a bit. Slowly cook for 5 to 7 minutes, until the sauce gets a little thicker.
2. Using a fine-mesh sieve, strain the sauce to get rid of any seeds. Let it cool down a bit before you serve it.

Decadent Finale:

1. Be careful when taking the puddings out of the steamer; let them cool for a few minutes.
2. Flip the puddings over onto plates and drizzle with the raspberry sauce, which can be warm or cold. Enjoy the contrast between the warm, fluffy dark chocolate pudding and the bright, sour raspberry sauce!

109. STEAMED BANANA MUFFINS

Prep Time: 15 minutes | Cook Time: 15-20 minutes

Total Time: 30-35 minutes

Servings: 12 muffins

Ingredients

Wet Ingredients:

- 1/4 cup of melted butter or coconut oil
- 2 ripe bananas, mashed
- 1 egg
- 1/4 cup of honey or maple syrup
- 1 tsp vanilla extract

Dry Ingredients:

- 1 1/2 cups of all-purpose flour
- 1/2 cup of chocolate chunks (milk, dark, or semi-sweet, as you prefer)
- 1 tsp baking powder
- 1/4 cup of chopped pecans
- 1/4 tsp salt
- 1/2 tsp baking soda

Instructions

1. For the muffin pan, put paper liners in it and heat up your electric steamer.
2. Break up the bananas into chunks and mix them in a big bowl. Add the honey or maple syrup, egg, melted butter or coconut oil, and vanilla extract. Stir the ingredients together until they are well blended.
3. Throw the flour, baking powder, baking soda, and salt into a different bowl and mix them together using a whisk. Combine the dry ingredients slowly with the wet ones, stirring only until everything is well mixed. Be careful not to mix too much!
4. The chocolate chunks and chopped pecans should be carefully mixed in.
5. Put the same amount of batter in each of the muffin cups that have been prepared. Three-quarters of the way full should be used. Cover the steamer basket and put the muffin pan inside it. A toothpick stuck in the center of a muffin should come out clean after 15 to 20 minutes of steaming.
6. Wait a few minutes before moving the muffins to a wire rack to cool completely. Although they are still warm, you can eat your steamed banana muffins with chocolate chunks and pecans cold.

110. STRAWBERRY AND RICOTTA STEAMED CREPES

Prep Time: 20 minutes | Cook Time: 12-15 minutes

Total Time: 27-30 minutes

Servings: 4-6 crepes

Ingredients

For the Crepes:

- 1 tbsp melted butter or vegetable oil
- 1 cup of milk
- 1/4 tsp salt
- 2 eggs
- 1 cup of all-purpose flour

For the Filling:

- 1 tsp vanilla extract
- 1/4 cup of honey or maple syrup
- 1 cup of fresh strawberries, sliced
- 1 cup of ricotta cheese

Optional Decorations:

- Drizzle of honey or maple syrup
- Fresh mint leaves
- Powdered sugar

Instructions

1. Mix the flour and salt together in a big bowl. Make a hole in the middle and put the eggs in it. Carefully whisk in the flour one tbsp at a time until a smooth batter forms. Add the milk slowly while whisking until everything is well mixed. Add the melted oil or butter and mix it in. Warm up your electric steamer. Put some oil on a steamer basket or put parchment paper inside it.
2. Put about a quarter cup of batter in the middle of the steamer basket that has been greased. Slowly swirl the batter to make a thin crepe. Remove the lid and steam for two to three minutes or until the edges are set and the middle no longer looks wet. Do it again with the rest of the batter, making sure there is space between the crepes so they can steam.
3. Whip the ricotta cheese, honey or maple syrup, and vanilla extract in a small bowl until smooth and creamy while the crepes are cooking.
4. Spread a small amount of ricotta filling on top of each crepe before putting them together. Add strawberry slices to the crepe, then fold it in half or roll it up.
5. Sprinkle with powdered sugar, add fresh mint leaves for decoration (if you want), and drizzle with more honey or maple syrup if you want. You can eat your steamed strawberry and ricotta crepes hot or cold.

111. STEAMED BAKLAVA WITH ROSEWATER

Prep Time: 30 minutes | Cook Time: 40-45 minutes

Total Time: 70-75 minutes

Servings: 8-10 pieces

Ingredients

For the Filling:

- 1 1/2 cups of shelled pistachios, finely chopped
- Pinch of salt
- 1/8 tsp ground cinnamon
- 2 tbsp rosewater
- 1/4 cup of granulated sugar
- 1/4 tsp ground cardamom
- 1/4 cup of melted butter

For the Dough:

- 1/2 cup of unsalted butter, softened
- 1/4 tsp salt
- 1/4 cup of water
- 1/4 cup of vegetable oil
- 1/4 tsp rosewater
- 1 1/2 cups of all-purpose flour

For the Syrup:

- 1/4 tsp rosewater
- 1/2 cup of water
- 1 cup of honey

Optional Decor:

- Chopped pistachios
- Powdered sugar

Instructions

1. Filling Symphony: Get your electric steamer ready to go. Put the chopped pistachios, sugar, cardamom, cinnamon, salt, melted butter, and rosewater in a bowl. After mixing well, set it aside.
2. Mix the flour and salt together in a different bowl. To make the butter and oil light and fluffy, mix them together with a hand mixer or a stand mixer. Add the flour mixture slowly while mixing in the water and rosewater one at a time until a soft dough forms. Refrain from mixing too much.
3. Split the dough in half. Use a little flour on a flat surface to make a thin sheet out of one-half of the dough. It needs to be about 1/8 inch thick. Cover half of the dough with the pistachio filling. Like a jelly roll, roll the dough up tight around the filling. Do it again with the rest of the dough and filling.
4. Cut each piece of rolled dough into a 1-inch slice. Make sure there is space between the slices on a plate or steamer basket lined with parchment paper so that they can steam. For 40 to 45 minutes, or until the baklava is fully cooked and a little golden brown, cover it and steam it.
5. Making the syrup will take some time while the baklava is hot. Put the honey, water, and rosewater in a saucepan and mix them together. Bring to a simmer and stir the syrup a few times to make it a little thicker. Let the syrup cool down a bit before you use it.
6. After steaming the baklava, pour a lot of the warm or cold syrup over it. Before you serve it, let it cool for at least 30 minutes so that the syrup can soak in and the flavors can mix.
7. For an extra touch of class, you can dust it with powdered sugar and, if you want, sprinkle it with chopped pistachios. Enjoy your Middle Eastern steamed baklava, which smells and tastes great.

112. JAPANESE GREEN TEA MOCHI WITH RED BEAN PASTE

Prep Time: 15 minutes | Cook Time: 15-20 minutes

Total Time: 30-35 minutes

Servings: 10-12 mochi

Ingredients

For the Mochi Dough:

- 2 tbsp matcha powder
- 2 tbsp vegetable oil
- 1/4 cup of water
- 1/4 cup of powdered sugar
- 1 cup of glutinous rice flour (mochiko)

For the Red Bean Paste (Anko):

- 1 tbsp powdered sugar (optional)
- 1/2 cup of store-bought red bean paste (anko)

Optional Decor:

- Powdered sugar
- Kinako (roasted soybean flour)

Instructions

1. Mix the powdered sugar, matcha powder, and glutinous rice flour together in a large bowl using a whisk.
2. Put the water and vegetable oil in a different bowl. Slowly add the wet ingredients to the dry ones while stirring all the time until a smooth dough forms. Gently knead the dough for a few minutes to make sure it's all mixed together.
3. Cut the dough into 10 to 12 equal pieces. Make a small ball out of each piece. Put a little oil on your steamer basket or put parchment paper inside it. Make sure the mochi balls don't touch as you put them in the basket. Put the lid on top and steam for 15 to 20 minutes or until the mochi balls are slightly puffed up and clear.
4. If you bought red bean paste, get it ready while the mochi is steaming. You can change how sweet the red bean paste is by mixing it with powdered sugar in a small bowl.
5. The mochi balls should be carefully taken out of the steamer and left to cool a bit after they are done. Put a little red bean paste inside each mochi ball and pinch the dough closed to hold the filling in place.
6. You can add extra flavor and texture to the mochi by dusting it with kinako or powdered sugar. Have a nice time with your steamed Japanese green tea mochi with red bean paste.

113. FRENCH STEAMED CLAFOUTIS

Prep Time: 15 minutes | Cook Time: 25-30 minutes

Total Time: 40-45 minutes

Servings: 4-6 clafoutis

Ingredients

For the Berries:

- 1 tbsp granulated sugar
- 1 1/2 cups of fresh berries (blueberries, raspberries, blackberries, or a mix)
- 1 tsp lemon juice

For the Custard:

- Pinch of salt
- 2 large eggs
- 1/4 cup of honey or maple syrup
- 1/4 tsp vanilla extract
- 1/2 cup of milk
- 1/4 cup of all-purpose flour
- 1/4 tsp ground nutmeg (optional)

Instructions

1. Take care to wash and dry the fresh berries. Put the nuts in a small bowl and add the sugar and lemon juice. Put away.
2. Add the eggs, milk, honey or maple syrup, vanilla extract, nutmeg (if you want), and salt to a large bowl. Use a whisk to mix the ingredients well. Slowly whisk in the flour until it is just combined. Be careful not to mix it too much.
3. Get your ramekins or baking dishes ready, and then divide the berries among them. Pour the custard batter over the berries slowly until they are almost full. Put the ramekins in the steamer basket that has been lined with parchment paper. When you stick a toothpick in the middle, and it comes out clean, the custard is done. Cover and steam for 25-30 minutes.
4. Before moving the clafoutis to a wire rack to cool completely, let them cool a little in the steamer. You can eat them warm or cold, and each bite will give you a burst of bright berries and a hint of lemon zest.

114. ITALIAN STEAMED RICOTTA CHEESECAKE

Prep Time: 15 minutes | Cook Time: 25-30 minutes

Total Time: 40-45 minutes

Servings: 4-6 cheesecakes

Ingredients

For the Cheesecake:

- 1 tsp vanilla extract
- 2 large eggs
- 1 pound ricotta cheese (whole milk for richer flavor)
- 1/4 cup of honey
- 1/4 cup of all-purpose flour

For the Topping:

- 1 tbsp lemon juice
- 1/4 cup of honey
- 1/4 cup of water
- 1 cup of fresh seasonal fruit (sliced strawberries, peaches, blueberries, etc.)
- Pinch of salt
- Fresh mint leaves (optional)

Instructions

1. To make the ricotta cheese smooth and creamy, mix the ricotta cheese, honey, eggs, vanilla extract, and salt in a large bowl. Add the flour slowly and carefully until it is just mixed in.
2. Spread the cheesecake mix out in the ramekins or baking dishes that you have already prepared. Put them in the steamer basket that has been lined with parchment paper. Place a toothpick in the middle of the cheesecake and remove it clean after 25 to 30 minutes. This means the cheesecake is set.
3. Making the honey glaze will take some time while the cheesecakes are steaming. Put the honey, water, and lemon juice in a small saucepan and mix them together. Bring to a simmer and stir it every so often until it gets a little thicker. Allow it to cool a bit.
4. It's best to let the cheesecakes cool in the steamer for a few minutes before moving them to a wire rack to cool all the way down. Spread some of the honey glaze on top of each cheesecake, and then add your favorite fresh fruits. Add fresh mint leaves if you want, and enjoy!

115. ORANGE BLOSSOM STEAMED RICE PUDDING

Prep Time: 15 minutes | Cook Time: 20-25 minutes

Total Time: 35-40 minutes

Servings: 4-6

Ingredients

For the Pudding:

- 2 cups of milk (whole milk for richer flavor)
- 1/4 cup of chopped pitted dates
- 1/4 cup of sugar
- 1/2 cup of white rice
- 1 tsp vanilla extract
- 1 tbsp orange blossom water
- 1/4 tsp salt
- Pinch of ground cinnamon (optional)

For the Topping:

- 1/4 cup of chopped pistachios
- Fresh mint leaves (optional)
- Additional orange blossom water (optional)

Instructions

1. Use a fine-mesh sieve to rinse the white rice until the water runs clear.
2. In a saucepan, mix the washed rice, milk, sugar, salt, dates, orange blossom water, vanilla extract, and (if you want) cinnamon. Over medium flame, bring to a simmer, and stir every now and then. Turn down the heat, cover, and let it simmer for 10 to 15 minutes, or until the rice is soft and the mixture has gotten a little thicker.
3. Put the warm rice mixture into the ramekins or baking dishes that you have already prepared. Put them in the steamer basket that has been lined with parchment paper. Put the lid on top and steam for 20 to 25 minutes or until the pudding is set and feels a little firm.
4. Before moving the puddings to a wire rack to cool completely, let them cool a little in the steamer. When the puddings are cool, add chopped pistachios on top of each one. If you want, you can drizzle more orange blossom water on top and add fresh mint leaves as a garnish. Serve the Moroccan Orange Blossom Steamed Rice Pudding with Dates and Pistachios, and enjoy its delicious smell and taste!

116. STEAMED FRUIT COBBLER WITH BERRIES, PEACHES

Prep Time: 20 minutes | Cook Time: 25-30 minutes

Total Time: 45-50 minutes

Servings: 4-6

Ingredients

For the Fruit:

- 1/4 cup of granulated sugar
- 4 cups of fresh or frozen berries (mixed, blueberries, raspberries, etc.)
- 1 tbsp cornstarch
- 1/2 tsp lemon juice (optional)

For the Biscuit Topping:

- 1/2 tsp baking soda
- 1 1/2 cups of all-purpose flour
- 1/4 cup of cold unsalted butter, cubed
- 1 tsp baking powder
- 1/4 tsp salt
- 2 tbsp granulated sugar
- 1/2 cup of butter milk

Optional Toppings:

- Whipped cream
- Powdered sugar
- Vanilla ice cream

Instructions

1. Warm up your electric steamer. Mix the sugar and cornstarch with the fruit of your choice in a large bowl. If you want to, add the lemon juice to the apples.
2. Mix the sugar, baking powder, baking soda, and salt with a whisk in a different bowl. You can use your fingers or a pastry cutter to cut the cold butter into the dry ingredients until the mixture looks like big crumbs. Add the buttermilk and mix it in until a soft dough forms.
3. In a dish that can go in the oven or be used to steam food, spread the fruit mixture out on the bottom. You need to leave space between the dough balls so that they can rise. Spread dough out on top of the fruit with spoons.
4. Put the dish in the steamer basket that has been lined with parchment paper. Put the lid on top and steam for 25 to 30 minutes or until the biscuit topping is fully cooked and golden brown. If you stick a toothpick into the biscuit, it should come out clean.
5. Let the cobbler cool down a bit before you serve it. It tastes great, hot or cold, with whipped cream, powdered sugar, or your favorite ice cream on top.

117. HONEY GLAZED CARROTS WITH PECANS

Prep Time: 10 minutes | Cook Time: 15-20 minutes

Total Time: 25-30 minutes

Servings: 4-6

Ingredients

- 1/4 cup of chopped pecans, toasted
- 1 tbsp olive oil
- 1 tbsp Dijon mustard
- Freshly ground black pepper, to taste
- 1 pound fresh carrots, peeled and trimmed
- 1/4 cup of water
- 1/4 cup of honey
- Pinch of salt

Optional Garnishes:

- Chives, chopped
- Fresh parsley, chopped
- Chopped dill

Instructions

1. After you wash and peel the carrots, cut them into any shape you want. You can use batons, julienne, slices, or even baby carrots.
2. Warm up your electric steamer. Put the cooked carrots and olive oil in a large bowl and toss them around. Put them in the steamer basket that has been lined with parchment paper. Put the lid on top and steam for 15-20 minutes or until the carrots are soft and crisp to your liking.
3. Bring the honey glaze to a boil while the carrots smoke. Put the honey, water, Dijon mustard, salt, and pepper in a small saucepan. Put the glaze on a medium-low heat and stir it around a few times to make it a little thicker.
4. After steaming the carrots, put them in a dish to serve. Pour a lot of the warm honey glaze over the food and toss it around to coat it all. Add the toasted pecans and the garnish of your choice (if you want). Electric Steamer Honey Glazed Carrots with Pecans are sweet and crunchy. Serve them warm and enjoy!

118. STEAMED YOGURT AND GRANOLA MUFFINS

Prep Time: 15 minutes | Cook Time: 15-20 minutes

Total Time: 30-35 minutes

Servings: 12 muffins

Ingredients

Wet Ingredients:

- 1 tsp vanilla extract
- 1/4 cup of melted butter or coconut oil
- 1 cup of plain Greek yogurt
- 1/4 cup of honey or maple syrup
- 1 egg

Dry Ingredients:

- 1/4 tsp sal
- 1 1/2 cups of all-purpose flour
- 1/2 tsp baking soda
- 1/2 cup of rolled oats (old-fashioned or quick)
- 1/2 cup of granola (your favorite kind)
- 1 tsp baking powder

Optional:

- 1/2 tsp grated zest of orange or lemon
- 1/4 cup of dried fruit (cranberries, raisins, blueberries)
- 1/4 cup of chopped nuts (pecans, walnuts, almonds)

Instructions

1. In a big bowl, stir the pumpkin puree, honey or maple syrup, egg, vanilla extract, and melted coconut oil or butter. Mix the ingredients together well with a whisk.
2. In a different bowl, use a whisk to mix the flour, oats, granola, baking powder, baking soda, and salt.
3. Combine the dry and wet ingredients slowly while stirring just until everything is mixed. Avoid mixing too much! Add the optional ingredients (nuts, fruit, zest) slowly while folding them in.
4. Evenly spread the batter into muffin pan liners that have been prepared. Position the pan in the steamer basket that has been lined with parchment paper. Stick a toothpick in the middle of one of the muffins and remove it clean. This should take 15 to 20 minutes.
5. Take the muffins out of the steamer and let them cool for a little while. Then, move them to a wire rack to cool all the way down. Eat your yogurt and muffins made with the electric steamer when they are cool.

119. SPICED PEARS WITH VANILLA BEAN SAUCE

Prep Time: 15 minutes | Cook Time: 20-25 minutes

Total Time: 35-40 minutes

Servings: 4-6 servings

Ingredients

For the Spiced Pears:

- 1/4 tsp ground ginger
- 1 cinnamon stick
- 1 cup of water
- 4 ripe pears (Bartlett or Bosc work well)
- 1/4 tsp ground nutmeg
- 1/4 cup of honey or maple syrup
- 4 whole cloves
- Pinch of salt

For the Vanilla Bean Sauce:

- 2 tbsp cornstarch
- 1 cup of milk (whole milk for richer flavor)
- Pinch of salt
- 1/4 cup of honey or maple syrup
- 2 tbsp cold water
- 1 vanilla bean, split and scraped

Optional Garnish:

- Whipped cream
- Powdered sugar
- Chopped walnuts or pecans
- Fresh mint leaves

Instructions

1. Get the pears clean and dry. Carefully cut out the middle, leaving the bottom hole for display. You can peel the pears if you want to, but leaving the skin on gives them a more rustic look.
2. Honey or maple syrup, water, cinnamon sticks, cloves, ginger, nutmeg, and salt should all be mixed together in a large saucepan. Over medium-low heat, bring to a boil. Carefully put the pears into the liquid that is simmering, making sure they are mostly submerged.
3. Prepare your electric steamer. Place the pot on a steamer basket lined with parchment paper and cover it. Put the pears in the steamer for 20-25 minutes or until a fork can go through them easily.
4. Take the vanilla bean sauce out of the fridge while the pears cool down. Heat the milk in a small saucepan with the vanilla bean pod that has been scraped clean. Mix the cornstarch and cold water together in a different bowl using a whisk until the mixture is smooth. Once the milk starts to simmer, take out the vanilla bean pod and add the cornstarch mixture slowly while whisking it in. Keep whisking the sauce until it gets a little thicker. Add the honey and salt or maple syrup and mix well.
5. Serve the warm pears with spices and the rich vanilla bean sauce on the side. For an extra touch of class, top with whipped cream, powdered sugar, chopped nuts, or fresh mint leaves. Enjoy the Electric Steamer Spiced pearls with Vanilla Bean Sauce, which smells great and tastes great.

120. STEAMED FRITTATAS WITH CHERRY TOMATOES

Prep Time: 10 minutes | Cook Time: 12-15 minutes

Total Time: 22-25 minutes

Servings: 12-16 mini frittatas

Ingredients

- 12-16 cherry tomatoes, halved
- Freshly ground black pepper, to taste
- 1/4 cup of grated Parmesan cheese
- 3 large eggs
- Pinch of salt
- 1/4 cup of milk (whole milk for richer flavor)
- 1/2 cup of fresh basil leaves, chopped

Instructions

1. In a big bowl, stir the eggs, milk, Parmesan cheese, salt, and pepper together using a whisk.
2. Add the cherry tomatoes cut in half and chopped basil leaves slowly.
3. Grease a mini muffin pan that can be used for steaming. Evenly spread the egg mixture into the molds that have already been made.
4. Warm up your electric steamer. Put the muffin pan in the steamer basket that has been lined with parchment paper. If you stick a toothpick in the middle and it comes out clean, the eggs are done. Cover and steam for 12-15 minutes.
5. Before moving the frittatas to a wire rack to cool completely, let them cool a little in the steamer. Enjoy your colorful and tasty Electric Steamer Mini Steamed Frittatas with Cherry Tomatoes and Basil once they are cool.

Printed in Great Britain
by Amazon